Baby Boomer Bust?

Baby Boomer Bust?

୧ৎ

How the generation of promise became the generation of panic.

ROGER CHIOCCHI

New York

Baby Boomer Bust?
How the Generation of Promise Became the Generation of Panic

ISBN 978-1-60037-751-8

Library of Congress Control Number: 2010920608

Morgan James Publishing
1225 Franklin Ave., STE 325
Garden City, NY 11530-1693
Toll Free 800-485-4943
www.MorganJamesPublishing.com

To Philomena: *may the lasting imprint of your spirit, your warmth, your loving soul and your innate capacity to always find the very best in people, be a legacy that remains with us forever.*

&

To Catherine: *never forget the lessons you learned from the best, most inspirational teacher one could ever have; may her legacy guide you throughout life.*

Acknowledgements

It was definitely an uncomfortable, anxiety-inducing feeling, akin to incessantly twisting back and forth in an undersized seat of a small commuter airplane after having been stuck on the runway for three hours with only sporadic updates from the crew. It was a complete loss of control, an unintended yielding of the forces ruling my life to an entity or entities I never in my wildest imagination would ever yield them to, a free-fall without having any knowledge at all of – or trust in – whoever's responsible for my safety net.

That's how I felt the day the Dow hit 6700 in spring of 2009.

I had been avoiding looking at my online statements for weeks, probably months. What was once a sense of moderate contentment in knowing that I'd be relatively okay going forward gradually became a sense of avoidance and, over time, outright fear.

GEEZ, how am I ever going to retire on that? I thought.

Soon this bewilderment grew into outright anger. *How dare those Wizards of Wall Street screw up the economy so bad, take federal money to bail themselves out, still reward themselves with big bonuses, while hanging everyone else out to dry?*

But, alas, like almost everyone else, I was helpless to do anything about it.

Until I decided to write this book.

At my company, Brandloft, one of our key competencies is conducting in-depth qualitative one-on-one interviews in our pursuit of making sense of an issue; when given a marketing issue we like to "surround" it with different stakeholder viewpoints and then analyze what's really going on from every possible perspective. *Why not apply this competency to our current economic crisis and its effect on the once vaunted Baby Boomer generation?* I thought.

Thus the genesis for *Baby Boomer Bust: How the generation of promise became the generation of panic.* From there, the book took on a life of its own: consuming most of my time as it ultimately was molded into three parts.

In Part I, I present the findings of an online qualitative survey where I share the views of our panel of 150 Baby Boomers on how the economy has affected their lifestyles, consumption patterns, their dreams and aspirations and, of course, who they believed caused it and how they feel about it; additionally, I try to give an explanation of the forces that caused the meltdown to happen in layman's terms.

Part II is the heart and soul of the book: Here I tell the stories of nine different baby boomers – from across the economic spectrum – and how they've been able to cope, or not, with the effects of the meltdown. You'll find their stories poignant, touching and, hopefully, thought-provoking.

In Part III, I try to suggest some solutions for the problems confronting Boomers going forward, particularly retirement, and take a look at the underlying issues – and some possible remedies for – the factors that caused the meltdown.

I'd like to thank Caron Knauer for her insightful editorial comments (constantly sending me back to the drawing board), Nancy Nisselbaum for her copyediting and Eileen DeVries for her legal input. My business partners at Brandloft, Ed Libonati and Mark Baxter, gave me the help, encouragement and latitude to pursue this dream. Victor DeCastro, art director extraordinaire, designed a wonderful cover. Dr. Ronald Manheimer, Michael J. Formica, Jerry Shereshewsky, Paul Arfin and Scott Adams provided stimulating input in their respective areas of expertise and Eileen Winters did a masterful job of researching some of the issues and identifying Baby Boomers to interview for Part II.

Most of all, though, I'd like to thank our nine Boomers and their families. In return for their candor, I've changed their names because, from early on, I felt strongly that this book was not about "exploiting" our subjects, but rather to use their stories to understand the consequences of the meltdown on a much deeper, more meaningful level. So, thank you, pseudonyms! Thank you Dick Shaughnessey, Donna Dellasandro, Kurt Simpson, Ian Stein, John Perrotti, John and Georgia Albee, Dan Besso and Scott Divak. You know who you are!

If the time I and my colleagues and our group of Boomers devoted to this book results in making one person think differently about the meltdown and its effect on our world, the time would have been very well spent, indeed.

Roger Chiocchi
Norwalk, CT

"What do you think becomes of people when
their civilization breaks up? Those who have brains and
courage come through all right. Those who haven't are winnowed out."

Ashley Wilkes to Scarlett O'Hara, after having lost their fortunes in
Gone With the Wind.

Contents

PART I

The Perfect Storm

Introduction

Wipeout

We've all seen the commercial. Dennis Hopper, an icon of the Easy Rider days of the 1960s, a poster boy for the "love generation," a.k.a. the Baby Boomers (although not technically one himself), is standing on a beautiful beach with calming azure blue water, warm soothing sands, white puffy clouds and a hint of an inviting, uninhabited island on the horizon. He's wearing a black collared shirt, a pair of ultra-cool, but understated, shades and sports a small salt-and-pepper goatee. Holding an old tattered dictionary, he reads the definition of the word *Retire*: "to withdraw, go away, disappear." Then in his inimitable, sort of aloof, but rebellious tone of voice, he announces, "Time to redefine."

He drops the dictionary on the beach and the music begins.

Bah-dah-dah-dah-dah-Bump. Bah-dah-dah-dah-dah-Bump.

With the opening chords to *Gimme Some Lovin'* by the Spencer Davis group—classic 1960s rock—pulsating underneath, Hopper goes on to tell us that, "Your generation is definitely not headed for Bingo night. In fact you can write a book about how you're going to turn retirement upside down."

In an odd sort of way, this is that book.

Unfortunately, it's not about turning retirement upside down in quite the way that Hopper and Ameriprise, the sponsor of the ad, envisioned. We're going to turn it upside down because most of us are pulling the collective hairs out of our heads in a state of outright panic and shock.

I wrote this book because, as a Boomer in his mid-50s, I thought I was reasonably well set for the future. I had enjoyed a successful career as a senior executive on Madison Avenue and as President of a medium-sized advertising agency in the East Village before I started my own small agency in Connecticut, where I could do my own thing and pursue my passion for writing (mostly fiction). Then, suddenly, the meltdown strikes and all my assets are cut in half. It forced me —and most of us Baby Boomers—to re-evaluate our preparedness for what lies ahead. We became disoriented because of the gap between our previous expectations and this new reality. *Baby Boomer Bust?* is all about the chasm between our generation's lofty expectations and that sobering reality that confronts us as we approach our 50s and 60s.

My purpose is to examine this chasm—this gap—to try to explain why it exists. Is it that our expectations were set much too high? Were our accomplishments much too modest? As a generation, did we allow the relationships between government, business and civility to get out of whack? Was the economic downturn of 2008/2009 the cause of our downfall, the effect of our downfall or merely a punctuation mark, wickedly accenting the failures of a generation?

Baby Boomer Bust? will examine this phenomenon from several perspectives. First, I'll present the findings of a panel of more than 150 Baby Boomers who we queried via an online survey. These respondents tell us how the downturn affected their lives, their consumption patterns, and their abilities to provide for their family's housing, their children's education and their own retirements. They'll tell us who they think is to blame for our current economic malaise and how it's affecting their political leanings. Finally, they'll tell us what they think the future has in store for us.

Next, the book will explain the causes underlying our economic state. Whether the downturn of 2008/2009 is, indeed, a cause, an effect or a punctuation mark, you'll find that the story is convoluted, complex and built on a foundation of greed.

Then the book will focus in even more. First, on five groups of individuals who responded to the survey in a like manner. Each group has its own set of quirks, although they all have a few things in common—mostly anger at the "system," however they define it, and uncertainty about the future.

At that point, we'll zoom in even closer, profiling eight individual Baby Boomers/families—their lives, experiences, careers, successes, failures, current economic status, views on the future and, most critically, how they are coping.

I'll share the stories of:

- Dick Shaughnessy. A telecommunications manager at Citigroup, he saw his 401K decrease by almost 70% as Citigroup stock nosedived from $50 to $2. Then to add insult to injury, he was laid off in October 2008.

- Donna Dellasandro. Once a relatively wealthy resident in one of the most affluent communities in America, she still lives there, but now is struggling to make ends meet.

- Kurt Simpson. A senior level marketing executive who, due to several extended hiatuses between jobs and multiple relocations, is virtually penniless although gainfully employed.

- Ian Stein. A successful broadcast journalist who's now living his dream of producing documentaries. It's a dream he's earned, but one that may be cut short by the failures of others.

- John Perrotti. Once a partner in a Wall Street trading firm who earned a high six-figure salary, today he's tending bar in a trendy Connecticut bistro.

- John and Georgia Albee. This New Jersey couple worked hard for 30 years to build a successful auto dealership and came within inches of losing it all because of the economic downturn's effect on Chrysler.

- Dan Besso. A retired police officer who has parlayed his pension and a small alarm company business into a decent life for himself and his family

- Scott Divak. An advertising copywriter who has been laid off time and time again, but who always finds the resiliency to come back.

I've changed the names—but not the stories—of these people because the intent of this book is not to exploit our subjects but rather to use their stories to illustrate the impact of the economic downturn on their lives as well as the key issues facing the Baby Boomer generation going forward.

Finally, in the last three chapters, I'll try to make sense of it all. I've interviewed experts on personal bankruptcy, retirement and psychology/sociology and cite other authoritative figures in an effort to provide perspective and, hopefully, some solutions.

But let's start at the beginning, the gap between what we expected and what we might end up with.

* * *

Chapter 1

The Expectation Gap

M ost of our parents had pensions, Social Security and the value of their homes to fund their retirements, creating a certain expectation in their children that our post-career lives would be somewhat comfortable as well. Unfortunately, our generation generally doesn't have pensions or defined-benefit retirement plans as formally defined (unless perhaps if you're a union worker or public employee), we've seen the value of our homes diminish, and even if Social Security—a sort of transfer payment from the next generation to ours—is still around when we need it, the maximum payment (currently about $3,000 per month) doesn't really excite anyone. Oh, yeah, and one other thing: Our cherished 401Ks and IRAs have tanked.

My colleagues and I conducted a survey of a broad spectrum of Baby Boomers in Spring 2009—when the effects of the economic downturn of 2008/2009 settled in, after the initial shock and numbing period of late 2008/early 2009. Because the online sample was not random, the results are not projectable to the entire population, but nonetheless, they provide us with a broad-scale qualitative snapshot of the feelings, behavior and the adjustments Baby Boomers made as a result of the downturn. (If anything, our panel was more upscale than the population at large, thereby giving us a good "acid test" of the impact of the recession.)

We asked our online panel many questions, but one of the most important was, "How do you plan to pay for your retirement?"

The sassiest answer? *The Lottery*

And what about housing? Our parents' generation practically went to the bank on the appreciation in the value of their homes. Could the Baby Boomers ride that escalator as well?

The bad news: Almost half of the people we talked to estimated that the value of their homes declined by 10% to 30% in the last 12 months.

The good news: Almost 60% of the Baby Boomers we talked to own their homes and think they will be fine in terms of being able to make their mortgage payments going forward. Surprisingly, only about 8% fear that their houses are "under water," meaning that the value of their home is less than the balance owed on their mortgage.

So with cautious optimism, it looks as if Baby Boomers will get some return on their housing investment. Of course, that's all dependent on the housing market coming back in future years, what they actually paid for their house and how long they've held it, how many refinancings they have been forced—*or will be forced*—to do, and, of course, their employment now and in the future.

As one Baby Boomer told us, despite the fact that their loan-to-value ratio is only at about 20%, "it's all dependent upon staying employed." Another added, "the answer is based on the condition of my husband's employment. With difficulty I could maintain my home with my present salary, but any cost increases would force me to sell it or find a second job."

And now for the coup de grace. We invested in a magical panacea called a 401K, which was designed to incent savings that would accumulate tax-free over the years and ride the never-ending rise of the stock market; at a mere 6% or 7% a year, our financial advisors told us, the cumulative value of what we stashed away would double every 10 to 12 years.

Mesmerized, we ogled at the spreadsheets. *Jesus Christ, honey! In 2020, our 401K will be worth $3 million. Maybe we should start looking for that little shingle-style bungalow with a water view on Nantucket.*

Emboldened by a 14,000 Dow in 2007, we upped the ante. *Geez, maybe that little bungalow should become a 5,000-square-foot waterfront McMansion.*

Then the bottom fell out.

The 14,000 Dow from 2007 became the 6,700 Dow in March 2009. Down more than 50%, which of course means that the Dow will have to *increase by more than 100%* just to get back to where it was in 2007.

Instead of that waterfront McMansion on Nantucket, we may have to settle for a modest retirement village in Nanuet.

Without doubt, the economic downturn of 2008/2009 has wreaked havoc on the lives, dreams, aspirations, consumption habits and net worths of our cherished Baby Boomer generation. We found a number of interesting and sometimes frightening themes in our survey of this vaunted generation.

Let's start by tackling the veritable 800-pound gorilla in the room— retirement.

A Less Than Idyllic Retirement

More than 30% of the Baby Boomers we talked to told us, "Frankly, I don't think I'll ever be able to retire." About 43% of them *thought* they were okay before the current economic downturn but now doubt their ability to retire based upon the current value of their assets.

A prevailing thought was expressed by one of our respondents: "The idea of retirement has become further and further away for the average and below-average citizens in this country." And another told us: "I will not be able to retire and maintain my present lifestyle."

According to Dr. Ronald Manheimer, former Executive Director of the NC Center for Creative Retirement at UNC Asheville, "There are several studies and surveys out there done by academic researchers and financial services companies that paint a dire picture of Boomers' ability to retire soon or ever. In the aggregate this is probably true though most will eventually retire either because they want to or have to. They will simply adjust…not painlessly, but resignedly. People will have to sell their homes and move into apartments or low-cost condos. They will have to find satisfaction and meaning in their later years through other means than greater wealth would have allowed."

Okay? So how bad is it really?

We asked our panel of Baby Boomers how they planned to fund their retirements. The leading sources were 401Ks (63%), Social Security (61%) Personal Wealth (41%, but that number is somewhat redundant with 401K and housing), and Sale of Existing Residence (35%). Only 28% mentioned that they had some sort of pension.

So exactly how adequate—or not—are these resources to fund a decent retirement?

I decided to address the point head-on by performing a simple analysis. Since our Boomers told us that Social Security, their 401Ks and selling their existing residences were their primary retirement funding vehicles, we took the *average value of these assets across the U.S.* and uncovered some interesting findings.

Let's say a Baby Boomer is 53 today—right smack in the middle of the Baby Boomer Bubble. Here's what they're looking at in terms of a monthly budget if they choose to retire at 62, 65 or 67. I performed the analysis under two different scenarios: a) selling their primary residence and b) keeping their primary residence.

Retirement Age (53 year old in 2009)	62	65	67
Monthly Budget if Primary Residence is SOLD	$4,342	$5,531	$6,334
Monthly Budget if Primary Residence is NOT SOLD	$3,200	$3,976	$4,428

This analysis was based upon a current 53-year-old having an average household 401K or IRA balance of $100K (which is generous; the Center for Retirement Research at Boston College estimates that the average family approaches retirement with only $60K in retirement savings), the national average current home value of $180,100 and a national average mortgage balance of $108,658. I allowed for an initial 15% bump in 2010 in home and 401K values (to allow for an initial recovery) and 6% a year thereafter. I also anticipated each household saving an additional $3K per year through retirement age and collecting the current maximum Social Security benefits (single wage earner household with benefits for non-working spouse) for their retirement age unadjusted for future Cost Of Living Adjustments. The total net worths (assuming both with and without the sale of their primary residence) were annuitized through age 87 at 6% annual growth. Finally, I assumed 25% for taxes and Medicare and/or health insurance. (NOTE: for age 65,the Full Retirement Age of 66 years and 2 months was utilized for the calculation of Social Security benefits).

The monthly budget numbers aren't draconian by any means— particularly in some regions of the country—but they are, by most standards, modest. So for most Baby Boomers the dream of retirement as that frolic on the beach with Dennis Hopper is exactly that—a dream.

No wonder 17% of Baby Boomers told us, "I plan to work until I drop because I have to."

So here's the retirement conundrum. Based on national averages, the monthly retirement budget predictably increases as you defer retirement. However, this implies that you have the ability to defer retirement, in other words, you manage to keep yourself employed, not an easy trick in today's economy.

But, if a large number of Boomers are lucky and manage to remain employed to 67—or even older—this could create a logjam at the entry level of the employment base, which, of course, would mean fewer people from subsequent generations contributing to the Social Security Trust. On the other hand, if a Boomer is laid off, he/she would be forced to dip into what otherwise would be their retirement savings to fund their living situation today. And, if they have children of college age? *WHAM! BAM! ZONK!*

Social Insecurity?

When we asked our Boomers about Social Security, one of them answered: "It's the largest Ponzi scheme going."

An interesting, although not completely accurate, analogy.

Ponzi schemes work as long as the base of the pyramid is wider than the peak. Frighteningly, the generation behind ours—the ones who will fund our Social Security payments—is smaller in number than our generation. So if Social Security is, indeed, a Ponzi scheme, we're in a lot of trouble. (In effect, we'd be being *Bernie Madoffed* by the U.S. government.)

Indeed, Social Security is probably one of the most misunderstood, if not anxiety-inducing, institutions in modern America. Is it a trust fund with our contributions stashed away in some mythical bank for us to collect when our time comes? Is it a transfer payment from one generation to another? Is it some sort of increasingly insolvent bubble that will one day burst just like the Tech Bubble of the 1990s and the Sub-Prime Mortgage Bubble of today? Or is it, indeed, "the world's largest Ponzi scheme?"

It seems as if most of us either don't really know, don't want to know or are just writing it off. As one Boomer put it, "I'm not counting on Social Security being around by the time I'm eligible to collect."

So what's the reality? Will Social Security be around for us Boomers to collect?

The news is really not so bleak. Social Security is *both* a transfer payment and a trust. As currently designed, the payroll tax of 12.4% (shared equally by employees and employers) more than covers the benefits doled out to retirees. The surplus is then put into a trust fund that is invested in government bonds.

So far, so good, right?

But here's the kicker. In the year 2017, projected total benefits paid will be *in excess* of payroll taxes collected. So Social Security will have to start supplementing the taxes with interest earned on the bonds in the trust fund. This may not be such a terrible fate; we'd live off bond interest, just like those "trust fund babies" most of us envy. (Author's Note: as this book was being written, it was reported that, due to lower payroll tax payments as a result of the recession, the surplus may actually be wiped out in 2010, seven years ahead of schedule; of course, if we have other "boom" years in the future, that can move things in the opposite direction. Accordingly, this analysis may swing a few years in either direction over time)

In 2027, though, projected benefits paid to retirees will be *in excess* of what can be financed by *both* the taxes collected *plus* the interest earned on the trust fund. Now at that point, we are going to be forced to commit the unpardonable sin of cutting into principal. We'll need to sell a portion of the bonds each year to make the benefit payments—not such a good idea.

In 2040, the trust fund is projected to be completely depleted and, if nothing is changed in the interim, the payroll taxes would have to be raised to 16.7%, a 35% increase, to fund the benefits paid to retirees. In 2082, the payroll tax would have to be raised to 17.8%.

So, with a little bit of luck, it looks like Social Security will be around for most of Baby Boomers' lifetimes. Various proposals have been made to either raise more revenues (one idea suggested was to invest the trust fund in equities instead of government bonds, which in hindsight is a not so good idea!) or decrease benefits NOW so as not to have to "fall off the cliff" in 2040. What's really frightening is that Social Security was designed to cover only a portion of a retiree's monthly budget (41% of pre-retirement earnings up to a designated cut-off), which begs the question: What happens when retirees run through their other sources of income? (Our examples in the previous section assumed that total net worth would be depleted by age 87.)[1]

So, to answer our original question, is Social Security truly a Ponzi scheme? Currently, three workers contribute for each retiree, but, again, right now Social Security is still generating a surplus (at least until 2010). By 2035, it will be two employees contributing per each retiree.[2]

You decide.

Impoverished Millionaires?

At the beginning of *Austin Powers: International Man of Mystery,* both secret agent Austin Powers and his nemesis, Dr. Evil, cryonically frozen in the 1960s, are thawed in the 1990s. Dr. Evil, up to no good, reveals he stole a nuclear weapon and immediately demands a ransom of *"One Million Dollars!"*

Cut to widespread bewilderment underscored by deadpan silence. (Later, when Dr. Evil realizes how times have changed, he ups his ante to $100 billion.)

Truth be told, a millionaire isn't a millionaire any more, but it certainly beats the alternative. Interestingly, or perhaps, predictably, many Baby Boomer millionaires don't feel so secure. Surprisingly, 18% of them described themselves as either "Compromised" or "Poor" as a result of the downturn.

And our Baby Boomer millionaires aren't too sanguine about their employment status either: 43% expressed some sort of discomfort with their current employment situation (including 7% who had recently been laid off and 2% who had to hold down several jobs to get by). Predictably, this had a ripple effect on their housing situations with 28% of our Baby Boomer millionaires expressing discomfort over being able to make their mortgage payments in the future.

And their retirement plans? 50% responded positively to, "Before the economy turned I thought I was fine. Now I'm not so sure." 17% went so far to say, "I never believed that my personal assets would be sufficient to pay for my retirement." Remember, these are *millionaires* saying that their personal assets are *NOT SUFFICIENT* to pay for retirement!

No wonder that 27% of our Baby Boomer millionaires expressed either a Significant or Overwhelming amount of stress in their lives due to the downturn.

"My job is at risk, so it colors my thinking and comfort level," one of them told us. Another confided, "I was downsized in January. Need to dip into savings until a new job is found." Then, the double-whammy: "Both my husband and I had jobs eliminated late last year."

Alternatively, we have our Back-to-Basics Boomer Millionaire who told us, "We are pretty frugal and derive our satisfaction in simple ways, so it hasn't been much of a change for us."

An interesting response that indeed proves the coin has another side: "I work for a university. Our enrollment is up 8%." Perhaps the reason enrollment is up is because overall employment is down, which begs the question, Is higher education a counter-cyclical growth industry?

Employment Angst

Worrying about staying employed is an anxiety not solely restricted to our millionaire Boomers. 47% of our total Boomers group expressed some sort of fear or discomfort about their employment status going forward:

- 12% claimed they worked for a big company and were worried about their jobs
- 2% were public employees who worried about their jobs
- 6% were recently laid off and are looking for new jobs
- 25% were self-employed and mentioned that business "was not so good"
- 2% told us they had to hold down several jobs to get by

Comments akin to, "My husband works for a modest-sized company and I would say his job is tenuous, too, because it's dependent upon the travel industry," or "I work for a small business and feel secure for now but I think I'll be laid off next winter if things don't pick up," and "Had to lay off most of the people who work for me and change assignments," or "I work for my town as an art instructor....I assume my job could be cut at any time," set the tenor of the group.

Another boomer told us, "We are towards the end of our earning potential. My husband and I are really feeling some major down-turns financially. We were forced to pay our taxes on credit cards—at 22%.... If we lose our house it will be the last one we own. My hubby is 56 years old....he now repairs metal roofs by himself. He cannot find someone to hire him outright...again, I emphasize a Baby Boomer is at the end of their earning potential. What now?"

However, all was not so bleak. Several Boomers told us that things were going quite well: "I'm actually turning down work, I'm so busy," and "I run a $4 million software company which is growing," and "I own an ad agency which has so far been relatively unscathed."

And, perhaps, the luckiest person of the bunch: "I have a pension."

The Socio-Tectonomic Shift.

If perception is reality, then self-perception is a deeper, albeit more subjective, form of reality. It affects our sense of self as well as our attitudes and opinions and, ultimately, influences behavior. So, with all this Boomer angst out there, we were interested in discovering how Baby Boomers perceived their socioeconomic status Pre- and Post-Downturn. We used Sept./Oct. 2008 (when the Dow plunged by over 25%, the AIG, Bear Stearns and CitiCorp disasters were coming to fruition and Paulsen and Bernanke were pitching the TARP program to Congress) as our demarcation date . Here's what we found:

Self-Perceived Socio-economic Status	PRE-Downturn	POST-Downturn	Difference
Rich	1%	2%	+1pt
Affluent	27%	14%	-13pts
Comfortable	50%	29%	-21pts
Okay	14%	22%	+8pts
Compromised	7%	26%	+19pts
Poor	< 1%	7%	+6pts

And the walls come tumbling down!

78% of our Boomers classified themselves as Comfortable, Affluent or Rich PRE-Downturn versus only 45% POST-Downturn. 8% classified themselves as Compromised or Poor PRE-Downturn whereas 33% put themselves in those categories POST-Downturn, a four-fold increase.

To put it in their own words:

"My husband was laid off from his manufacturing job that he had for 32 years. He is 59 years old. Too young to retire and probably too old to find employment in today's economic crisis."

"My job is at risk, so it colors my thinking and comfort level."

"One income earner left. Struggling with three children, mortgage, college tuition, etc."

"Self-employed and struggling to make it work. Could not find a job in my industry so did for myself."

Without doubt, this tectonic shift in perceived socioeconomic status has taken its toll on Boomer psyches. 35% of our Boomers—more than one-third!—told us they feel either a "Significant" or "Overwhelming" amount of stress and anxiety.

Reasons for this stress and anxiety run the gamut, from the dollars and cents ("My Merrill Lynch account dropped by $42K in January, $40K in February, and $26K in March. At my age, I will never recoup those losses.") to the real ("When I was laid off and looking for another job, I was miserable.") to the abstract ("[general] anger at the financial services community and the bailout.") to the anticipated ("I worry about my husband…he works for a large corporation…that has already completed two rounds of layoffs.") to the overall mood of the times ("the doom and gloom mentality around us affects my point of view.").

Perhaps the most poignant comment we heard regarding stress was, "It feels like trying to catch water, always slipping through your hands."

It reminded me of the tale of Sisyphus from Greek mythology—the poor soul who, as punishment for tricking the gods, was sentenced to roll a large boulder up a hill, only to have it slip out of his hands as he approached the top, rolling back down to the bottom and forcing him to start all over again.

Anxiety inducing, indeed!

Freedom's Just Another Word for Nothing Left to Lose?

So how has this anxiety affected our everyday lives?

According to Michael J. Formica, a Connecticut-based psychotherapist, social scientist and educator, "A great deal of what I'm seeing is what I refer to as 'things coming out sideways.' Situations that would typically remain contained under more normal circumstances are coming out in a much more destructive manner. Alcoholics are picking up. Drug addicts are falling back into old patterns. And I'm also seeing a real increase in anger management issues – things like domestic violence and road rage – that are escalating into police and court involvement."

Formica noted that there was also a positive side to the anxiety caused by the downturn. "I've seen an increase in marriage counseling. People are trying hard to make their primary relationships work because they simply cannot afford to divorce. It doesn't matter what the motivation is, they are prioritizing and becoming re-invested."

"I've also seen a decrease in extramarital affairs," Formica added. "People are both quitting their lovers and entering into counseling to help them step away from an on-going affair in order to work toward improving their situation at home. The New York Times actually recently published an article noting both of these trends."

Formica, who has practices in both very upscale and middle-class communities in Connecticut, notices a marked difference in the way that the very wealthy, wage earners and what he refers to as "blue collar professionals" react to the stress induced by the impact of the economic downturn. He cited the examples of a contractor with a degree in engineering that was forced to declare bankruptcy and is now working as a day laborer for a stone mason, as well as the case of a doctoral level chemist who lost his job with a large pharmaceutical company and now works at Starbucks and Blockbuster.

Contrastingly, he cited the example of a very wealthy stay-at-home mom with an MBA from a top business school that lost her multi-million dollar fortune due to the market downturn. "She's essentially doing everything she used to do – keeping the kids in private school, going to the club, regularly eating in restaurants, traveling constantly -- but she won't go back to work, enter into a situation that she perceives is below her previous station or do anything that would indicate her circumstances have changed. Her position is actually pretty common in this neck of the woods."

Denial, perhaps?

Formica disagrees. "It's more like a deficit in skills for the affluent," he said, "as well as a certain amount of social paralysis. In the case of this person, it's as if she simply doesn't know what to do, or even how to do things differently."

He suggests that wage earners and blue collar professionals, on the other hand, have a better set of tools to weather the storm. "They appear to be more resilient, and willing to set aside their ego to cut corners and make things work."

Consumption Patterns: That's so Dubai!

Given this dramatic shift in perceived socioeconomic status and the stress levels that it has apparently generated, we were interested in learning how the economic downturn is affecting Baby Boomers consumption activity, so we queried our group on any changes in spending across a spectrum of categories. We found some interesting, if not surprising, patterns.

Basically, we found consumer goods consumption falls into three categories: "Luxury Items," "Cheap Thrills" and "Essentials," each with its own unique usage pattern.

Luxury Items (Vacations, Leisure Activities, Meals Out at Restaurants, Wardrobe) all have been cut back substantially. 49% of Boomers told us they either "Eliminated Completely" or "Significantly Cut Back" their vacation plans; 44% claimed the same for Meals Out at Restaurants; and 41% said the same for Wardrobe Purchases.

One respondent summed it all up when she told us, "We're going to cut back. Anna Wintour was recently quoted at an ostentatious fashion show, 'That's so Dubai.' In other words, *that's so over.*"

Another told us, "I haven't been to the beauty salon for over a year! I've been cutting my own hair and it isn't pretty."

It's a well-known anecdote that movie attendance skyrocketed during the Great Depression. Our Boomers indicate a similar response today in what we call our "Cheap Thrills" categories—Movies, DVD Rentals, Premium Cable TV, Video on Demand and Health & Beauty Aids. 61% claim either an "Increase," "No Change" or only a "Slight Cutback" in movie attendance. An even more impressive 74% indicate the same response regarding DVD Rentals, Premium Cable and Video on Demand whereas 60% responded similarly when queried on Health & Beauty Aids consumption. As is the case in most economic downturns, consumers are substituting less-expensive satisfying experiences for their more expensive alternatives.

One of our Boomers gave us a pretty rational explanation of his household's current consumption activities: "We placed ourselves on an austerity but not bunker mentality plan."

Then, of course, there are the "Essentials," those items we simply cannot live without. 87% indicated either an "Increase,"" No Change" or a "Slight Cutback" in Medicine/Pharmaceutical consumption, 77% to Grocery consumption (although it would be interesting to see how their "mix" of groceries has changed) and 75% indicated a similar response regarding Alcohol and Tobacco consumption, two truly addictive behaviors.

"All non-essential expenses were reduced significantly or eliminated," one recently laid-off Boomer told us. Even insurance-covered doctor visits were cut back by one Boomer because of the co-pays.

In terms of Durable Goods, only 22% of Boomers went on and purchased as planned. Surprisingly, only 6% "downsized" the make/model of their purchase (indicating Boomers would still rather wait for the BMW than settle for the Honda). 19% indicated they concluded they didn't need the item after all.

The good news? 41% of Boomers said they would be deferring durable goods purchases until things get better, indicating a potential wave of pent-up demand once the economy recovers, which, of course, would help boost the recovery even more.

Comments by most of our Boomers stuck to the same hymnal:

"The 46-inch flat-screen will have to wait."

"No point spending what we have. A bigger TV doesn't make me happy."

"Does one need more than one of everything?"

"I will not purchase anything for which I cannot pay cash. If a commodity isn't needed, I won't purchase it."

Then, of course, there's the counter-intuitive response, although not without rationale: "I feel the need to purchase now while we have the funds versus later when our situation may be different."

Mad as Hell

So, let's see, so far our Boomers have seen their 401Ks and home values tank, they're worried about their jobs, their self-perceived socioeconomic status has gone down, their stress levels are up and they can't consume like they used to.

So it shouldn't come as a big surprise that they're mad as hell.

Truly, their anger is directed at everyone. But if we had to set our crosshairs on any one culprit, it would certainly be mortgage companies. 80% of Boomers cite mortgage companies as being "Very Responsible" for the downturn with 66% of Boomers claiming they are "Furious" at these companies.

"Many homeowners who bought what they could not possibly afford were truly duped into it. The mortgage lenders were often the culprit here," reflected the sentiments of many. Another Boomer told us, "Banks have to do their due diligence prior to making the loans. The home buyer that did not qualify should have never been given a loan."

Next in line as the focal point of our anger: Investment Bankers (80% of Boomers cited them as "Very Responsible," 56% were Furious at them), Wall St. ("Very Responsible" = 80%; "Furious" at = 54%), Hedge Fund Managers ("Very Responsible" = 75%; "Furious" at = 56%) and Large Multinational Banks ("Very Responsible" = 73%; Furious at = 43%).

Our Boomers were not shy in expressing their opinions about this lofty group:

"Treating homes as casino chips was a poor idea and packaging loans into traded derivatives was destructive. A bank that has no relationship with a borrower over the long term has no incentive to make sure the borrower can afford the loan and to work with the borrower through hard times."

"It's infuriating that Wall St. sold the nation down the river. How do we pay back a $12 Trillion debt?"

"Really mad at Wall St., big banks, investment firms and mortgage companies. They were all very irresponsible."

"I watched 30-year-old bond salesmen make over $1 million a year. It had to end. Finance sector in 2007 accounted for 35% of private sector profits. In 1982 it was 12%. Wall St. got rich while the nation struggled."

"This is truly the result of relentless fiscal irresponsibility and unmitigated greed. This was all about rich for the few and to hell with the middle class and the underserved."

Then, of course, there's government. The Bush Administration took its share of the blame as 72% of Boomers thought they were "Very Responsible" for the downturn and 42% said they were "Furious" at the previous administration. "The Bush Administration sunk this country due to lack of regulation," one Boomer told us.

Another treated Bush, Cheney and their crew with anything *but* kid gloves: "Bush & Co. broke the world. But they don't need to worry about retirement because they're raking it in with their investment in the oil industry, which raped us last summer. I think it's disgusting that Bush and Wall St. and all those other investment companies got away with their criminal acts for so long."

What was interesting, though, was the intensity of the reaction to the Clinton Administration. While only 29% cited the Clinton Administration as "Very Responsible" and only 15% said they were "Furious" at our 42nd President, they were quite a vocal minority:

"The Clinton Administration pushed for home ownership for more Americans. Barney Frank is hugely responsible."

"Fannie and Freddie pushing banks to get everyone in a house whether they could afford it or not."

It's quite possible that the Clinton Administration was being using as a whipping boy for the Democratic Congress as many of our Boomers' comments were pointed in that direction:

"The Democratic Congress was warned about this and they brushed it under the rug stating 'Things are fine.'"

"The liberals in Congress need to take the blame for much of this. And the left wing media for scaring people to death."

In terms of blame and feelings, the Boomers are pretty forgiving of the Obama Administration ("Very Responsible" = 10%; "Furious" = 8%). Their feelings run the gamut from acknowledgment that he had nothing to do with it, to suspicion that he's going to turn the U.S. into a socialist society, to outright hope that he can be a larger-than-life FDR-like figure who saves us from our downfall.

One Baby Boomer expressed the prevalent opinion that, "Obama was just elected, so his administration can't be responsible yet. We'll know in three years if Obama fixed things or made them worse."

Another Boomer told us, "I think Obama is working very hard to improve an unbearable inherited situation," while others were even more optimistic: "I have a lot of confidence, however, in the Obama Administration," and "Still I'm optimistic that I'll survive and eventually things will get better. And I have hope that the Obama administration will help turn things around."

However, there was also a degree of impending fear that the Obama administration might get *too involved*: "Obama socialism is an opportunistic overreaction that will promise a lower standard of living for future generations."

"Obama is making it a crime to receive a bonus or a good salary. He is trying to destroy those who earn money and pay most of the taxes in this country," was the opinion of another.

And last but not least, there are the poor souls who are smack at the center of this crisis: the homeowners who bought beyond their means. Our Boomers were somewhat forgiving of this group, particularly relative to the mortgage companies that overburdened them with debt and the financial institutions that minced their loans up into all sort of mystical financial products, with 60% saying these homeowners were "Very Responsible" and only 25% admitting that they were "Furious" at this group.

Perhaps one of our Boomers treated these homeowners with kid gloves because she was wary of living in a glass house: "Shouldn't those people have known they couldn't afford those houses? I think mortgage companies pushed aside their worries. You can't live like things will always go up. Everyone has been living that way. Me included. Hard lesson."

"If proper controls and standards were in place, 'Homeowners who bought houses they know they couldn't afford' would not be an issue," another told us, partially exonerating our over-extended homeowners.

Others were not nearly as forgiving: "I've been fiscally responsible and now I'm supporting the slackers. Yeah, I know, the house next door is on fire and do I want the fire to spread to mine? NO. But it's not fair."

Is this anger we see a good thing?

According to psychotherapist Formica, it's a double-edged sword. "Anger is what I call the *first feeling*," he explained. "It's a visceral response driven by a primal wiring around survival, safety, and sense of security. People regarded Wall Street and the financial community as something of a constant in their lives -- it was always there, providing a sense of social security through financial reward. Now that constant is gone."

He equates the situation to an individual who has gone to the same stream every day for water. One day when he arrives, the stream is dry. How is he going to react -- sulk over the loss of his source of water, or do something creative to rectify the situation?

"Anger becomes productive only when people can look past it, Otherwise, it's paralyzing," Formica explains. "If people unpack their anger and figure out how to move forward through it, it can be quite productive. Otherwise, you get more and more tied up, and then mired in the *emotion* – the *anxiety* – that drives the *feeling* – the *anger* -- rather than finding a way to do something creative in addressing the cause of the disturbance. That's how we can get stuck."

Without doubt, there was much anger expressed by our group of Boomers, some of it rifled at specific despised targets and some of it shotgunned out into space at no target in particular. One of our more interesting comments:

"Most people in government and executive positions are immoral. Until that changes, our country will go downhill. 'The Fall of Rome.'"

* * *

Chapter 2

So How Did We Get Into This Mess? —a Tragicomedy of Greed, Avarice, Deceit, Idealism and Horror

T*he Fall of Rome?* Perhaps a bit of an exaggeration, but, then again, maybe not.

A better analogy might be the destruction of the old South, as depicted so brilliantly in *Gone With the Wind.* At the end of Part I, we see Scarlet O'Hara, once a wealthy young darling of the South living life on a flourishing plantation, now broke, but not broken, standing before the vestiges of what was once her beloved *Tara*, promising that "with God as my witness, I will never go hungry again!"

A fitting analogy for the millions of boomers who find their budgets stretched, their savings depleted and their house under water these days. However, the cause of Scarlet's condition was very straightforward—the Civil War and the invasion of Georgia by General Sherman. The causes of our current predicament are much more difficult to grasp.

There is quite a lot of blame to go around and quite a lot of us doing the blaming. But what really happened? How did we get ourselves into this mess? If a screenwriter pitched a script about all this to the

Hollywood studios, it probably would be rejected outright. *Why?* It's too complex, too hard to follow, too long and too expensive.

But I thought I'd try anyway. Look at the situation as Hollywood might, except this is a story of such epic proportion, we need to string together segments from other big Hollywood epics to help us tell the story. So here we go:

The protagonists: our standard Baby Boomer couple, riding the Baby Boomer Bubble through a happy middle-class existence, striving to earn a decent living to make a home for their family, educate their kids and some day be rewarded with a decent retirement.

The antagonists: a complex web of greed-infested Gekkos from government and business who have an incessant need to squeeze dollars and cents from our protagonists to feed their never-ending hunger for money.

The conflict: it's a zero-sum game. Our Gekkos can only feed their greed at the expense of our Boomer couple.

FADE IN.

Scene 1: Wall St. "Greed is good." We open circa 1980, just as the Reagan years begin, as supply-side economics and the trickle-down effect become part of the *vox populi.* Cut to Gordon Gekko in *Wall Street* delivering his memorable "Greed Is Good" speech, sort of borrowing from the Invisible Hand idea espoused by Adam Smith several centuries earlier. *And what if one has to be ruthless, mean and backstabbing to achieve your greedy goals?* a young trainee innocently asks Mr. Gekko?

With a smirk, Gekko answers, "If you want a friend, buy a dog."

Scene 2: Mr. Smith Goes to Washington. Fast Forward to 1992: a young innocent man (okay so we're taking a little bit of license here) from the rural hinterlands comes to Washington. He's idealistic, progressive, wet behind the ears, represents a new generation and never stops "thinking about tomorrow." Just as the Jimmy Stewart character thought it would be a good idea to dedicate some land in his home state so that young boys could have a camp to go to, our Mr. Smith wants to do something good for his people, too—he wants everyone to be able to achieve the American dream of home ownership. Together with his friends Fannie and Freddie, he devises a plan.

But it turns out he wasn't as innocent as we thought (we won't mention incidents of a more salacious nature); in his intent to move his government to the center, he signs some deregulation legislation of dubious origin.

Scene 3: The Color of Money. Under scandalous circumstances, our 1990s version of Mr. Smith leaves town. However, because of a thriving business environment during his time in office, he's able to leave us in good financial shape. The country's budget is running a surplus, debt is being paid down and Social Security is funded well into the future.

But now there's a new sheriff in town, a cowboy from Texas (via Connecticut) and his sidekick (or vice versa) from Wyoming. They are the darlings of the Gekkos from the 1980s, who have now grown into true Masters of the Universe, with wealth and riches far beyond anyone's expectations. So what do the new sheriff and his sidekick decide? *Let's take the budget surplus and give it back to the Gekkos, our wealthy friends!* they proclaim. *And this regulation stuff?* They chortle, *Where we come from we don't like too many rules. Yee-hah!*

Scene 4: The Wizard of Oz. "Pay no attention to that man behind the curtain." As all this is going on in Washington, our Boomer couple is frolicking down the yellow brick road of life trying to achieve a modest degree of success for themselves and their family. Yet they are attracted to this magical vision on the horizon— it's fluorescent green, glows beautifully and promises them fabulous riches: great homes to live in and extra money to live on, mostly thanks to our modern-day Mr. Smith's friends, Freddie and Fannie.

All they need to do to partake in this bounty is meet with the Wizard and sign on the dotted line. He'll then make wonderful things happen for them, albeit with 95% Mortgages, No Income Verification Loans, Cash Back Refinancing and Low Adjustable Rates. But *yikes!* After jumping through hoops, our Boomers discover that this Wizard is not a Wizard at all, just a washed-up old carnival barker.

Unfortunately, by then, they're already hooked.

Scene 5: Frankenstein. "It's alive." As the Wizard was making his wonderful promises and easy loans to our Boomer couple, the Gekkos, or Masters of the Universe, bring out their mad scientists. These scientists are brilliant but not cute and sociable, sort of the Igors of Wall Street.

Just like Dr. Frankenstein sliced up corpses and sewed together different body parts to create his monster, these mad scientists sliced up the Wizard's loans and sewed them together into all sorts of exotic creatures, which they aptly named Sub-Primes. And just like Dr. Frankenstein's monster, these Sub-Prime creatures are destined to take on lives of their own and, ultimately, became impossible to control.

Scene 6: The China Syndrome. As the Sub-Prime creatures grow, a fusillade of money burrows right through the core of the Earth. It's source? China. This torrent of money—much of it earned on American exports—gobbles up American debt, mostly Treasury Securities, but, actually, a little bit of it goes to feed the Sub-Primes as well.

With all this cash in the system, the Wizard can sell more and more easy loans to more and more unsuspecting Boomer couples, giving them excess dollars to spend, which will eventually work their way back to China, only to be lent back to America, fueling even more growth. As the economy grows and the Wizard makes more loans, the mad scientists create even more Sub-Primes, in all shapes and sizes.

Scene 7: Gone With the Wind. The Sub-Primes get bigger and bigger and bigger—bubbling up, so to speak—as they feed voraciously on all the dollars in the system. And then they mate, creating a "master race" of Toxic Sub-Primes.

Fully grown, this bubbled-up strain of Toxic Sub-Primes, now on steroids, goes mad and begins to attack our homeland, just as General Sherman and his troops ravaged Atlanta. Cherished institutions come tumbling down, affluent friends of our Baby Boomers, and dare we say, our Baby Boomer couple themselves, are put out of work. Then a Carpetbagger from the North (well actually Washington, D.C., via New York) enters the scene. He tells us that the Toxic Sub-Primes have turned on the Gekkos, their creators. The government needs money from the Boomers—our tax dollars—and the Chinese to save the Gekkos and remove the Toxic Sub-Primes. The Boomers pause to scratch their heads, *Are you asking us to give you our hard-earned tax dollars so you can give more money to the Gekkos to save them from a problem they themselves created? Are we rewarding them for failure?*

Amid destruction and devastation, Boomer couples all across the country begin wondering, Is life as we know it *Gone With the Wind?* At the end of our movie, our Boomer wife, Scarlett—under water because of a bad loan granted by the Wizard, her husband out of work due to his company's devastation by the Toxic Sub-Primes—looks out upon the ravaged homeland and proclaims that famous line, "With God as my witness, I will never go hungry again!"

What a dramatic ending, a real cliff hanger!

But still the question remains: is it true, will she *really* never go hungry again?

FADE TO BLACK.

So there it is, the story of our crisis: **The Toxic Sub-Prime Bubbles That Ate America.**

Now for the credits:

Starring:

Greed/Wall Street (as themselves). Clearly, this is where it all began, the backdrop against which our tragicomedy plays itself out. "Greed is good" had become the mantra of the Wall Streeters in the 1980s, their inflated salaries justified because they were the ones, the true Masters of the Universe, who fueled the economy's growth, its effects trickling down to the masses.

True or not so true?

Interestingly, I came across a study by Thomas Philippon of NYU and Ariell Reshef of the University of Virginia regarding Wall Street wages relative to the rest of the private sector. They discovered something very insightful. During the last century, Wall Street wages exhibit a U-shaped curve relative to other private sector wages. And guess what? The largest premiums for average Wall Street (financial sector) salaries vs. other comparable private sector salaries—nearing 50%—were for the periods from 1909 to 1930 and from 1990 to 2006, the eras immediately preceding the Great Depression and the Sub-Prime meltdown of 2008/2009. Both of these periods were considered under-regulated or, at the very least, not competently regulated. During the period from 1950 to 1990, a more-regulated period of not-too-shabby growth, albeit with a few bumps in the road, Wall Street wages were almost on par with other comparable private sector wages. Furthermore, Philippon and Reshef went on to say that based upon their analysis of all the factors, one can conclude that "financiers are overpaid."[1] What does this say to us? *When too few people are making too much money with too little government regulation, the walls (pun fully intended) will come tumbling down!*

Mortgage Companies (as the Wizard). Traditionally the mortgage industry was considered a bit staid; that is, until the perpetually-tanned, snappy-dressing, Rolls Royce-driving Angelo Mozilo and his company,

Countrywide Finance, came to the forefront. A consummate salesman (one can even say Wizard, a metaphor for all of those high-performing mortgage salespeople in the early 2000s), Mozilo oozed entrepreneurial zeal and drive and was single-mindedly focused on one paramount goal—making his company the largest in the industry, an aspiration he achieved. By 2004, Countrywide became the number one originator of mortgage loans in the U.S., gobbling up market share from its competitors.

How did it do it? By requiring less loan documentation and by dangling low teaser rates at homeowners (which would eventually increase considerably), practices that would become rampant throughout the industry. But in 2007, the bottom fell out. Countrywide posted losses of $3.9 billion, eventually being bailed out by Bank of America. However, just prior to the losses, Mozilo began selling his Countrywide shares. Perhaps Mozilo knew something that the average shareholder did not; perhaps, despite being only a pseudo-Wizard, Mozilo could nonetheless foretell the future.

Pay no attention to that man behind the curtain, indeed!

Investment Bankers/Hedge Funds (as the mad scientists). As more and more of these sub-prime mortgages were being made, investment banks and hedge funds devised a scheme to allow banks to sell off their loans (and, for all practical purposes, their relationship with the borrower and the assumption of the risk) and package them into a bond-like object called a Collateralized Debt Obligation (CDO). This allowed the bank to take the money it received from the sale of the mortgage to make more loans, which on the surface seemed like a good thing. It also moved the loan from the more regulated banking industry to a less regulated environment with, in effect, fewer capital requirements and more opportunity for leverage. But it wasn't that the investment banks and hedge funds just took the loans and bundled them into a simple CDO; instead they cut up the loans into "tranches" determined by risk level. The first 50% of a loan might be in one tranche, the next 25% might be in another (or even in another CDO completely) and the last 25%—the riskiest, which would also pay investors the highest yield—might be in a third. This then became multiplied when mutual funds would buy up different tranches at different risk levels. A mutual fund made up of the riskiest tranches of many different CDOs might be completely wiped out if the underlying mortgages experienced a small increase in the level of defaults.

Another complicating factor was that the mad scientists of Wall Street would use a complex mathematical formula known as the *Gaussian copula,* developed by mathematician David X. Li, to model the risk and reward of these CDOs and ultimately set their prices. However some of these models failed to accurately estimate the risk of widespread default on the underlying mortgages.[2] It seems as if the rating agencies misjudged the risk/reward of these CDOs as well, giving some CDOs of questionable quality AAA ratings.[3]

Now add this to the mix that investment firms began issuing instruments called Credit Default Swaps (CDSs), which was basically an "insurance policy" that a loan would not default. Here's how it might work: I own a CDO. I go to a company like AIG and buy a CDS against my holding. I pay them an annual fee (an insurance premium) to insure me against the risk that the underlying loans will default. If the loans default, the insurance company pays me. Sounds simple and, in many ways, good. However, there were several problems with CDSs.

First, the CDSs could be traded in a relatively unregulated secondary marketplace. So the "buyer," the CDO holder, could sell his interest to a speculator, someone who didn't actually own the underlying CDO. The speculator would then pay the premiums to the issuer and effectively *bet against* the future of the housing market, hoping the underlying mortgages would fail and he would one day collect the insurance payoff. *Think of that, some speculator short selling your cherished home's mortgage!* But it gets better: The issuer—in this example, AIG—could sell its interest as well. The problem here, though, is that there were very lax controls and capital requirements in the secondary market. So there was no guarantee that the secondary holder of the CDS would have the capacity to pay if the underlying mortgages failed. Here's an analogy for you: *How would you feel if you found out that your home insurance company sold your policy and shifted the obligation to pay your claim should your house burn down to the local loan shark or bookie?*

Second, different CDSs would be bundled into funds. Since a CDS was not a conventional asset—it was considered a derivative—these funds were called "synthetic funds." Think of what might happen if hundreds of the riskiest of these exotic instruments were bundled in one highly leveraged fund with questionable capacity to make good on the claim and then the underlying loans failed.

So what happened? In their striving to create more and more exotic instruments with higher and higher yields—CDOs and CDSs combined mystically into all sorts of mutual funds and hedge funds—the system went awry. No one knew who held anything anymore. What were all these different exotic instruments worth? It was as if the "geeks," the backroom mathematicians who sliced and diced the underlying mortgages, bundled them into CDOs and assessed the risk and return on these assets, had outsmarted the "suits," according to Arnold King of the Cato Institute in his testimony before the House Committee on Oversight and Government Reform.[4] When the default and foreclosure levels on the underlying mortgages went up even slightly, the ripple effect would be multiplied exponentially throughout all these exotic assets, forcing their holders to write down the values on their balance sheets, in many cases billions and billions of dollars. As the underlying assets became riskier, holders were forced to raise their capital requirements, a margin call, so to speak. There was a problem, though. The security holders, in many cases, either didn't have or couldn't raise the capital.

And the further ripple effects? Less liquidity and credit throughout the economy, less promising business prospects, more layoffs, higher unemployment, lower home prices, a lower Dow and lower 401K values. *Yes, the walls did come a-tumbling down!*

It reminds me of a poignant scene at the end of the movie *Wall Street*, in which Bud Fox, the Charlie Sheen character, once Gordon Gekko's young golden boy, has a discussion with his father (in this case his real-life father, Martin Sheen), a blue-collar airline mechanic. A deal has just blown up in Gekko's face and it looks like poor Bud will have to go to jail for securities law violations. In a contemplative moment, Bud's father, confused about what they actually do on Wall Street, trading complex pieces of paper versus more traditional blue-collar occupations, gives his son some sound fatherly advice, "Stop going for the easy buck and produce something with your life. *Create, instead of living off the buying and selling of others.*"

Our Boomer Couple (as themselves). Our protagonists, the Baby Boomer couple: slightly upper-middle class, college educated, employed and with a couple of kids. *What's life been like for them?* Well, in many ways, it *is* sort of a stroll down the yellow brick road, replete with wonderful surprises, dangling temptations and threatening obstacles. Basically, our Boomers have tried hard to successfully navigate their families around this pathway of life's milestones—marriage, pregnancy, home ownership, getting the kids through school, then on to higher education—while still ending up with something for themselves.

Every day, they're bombarded by the signs of conspicuous consumption: luxury automakers promising them 0% financing (isn't that an oxymoron?), credit card companies filling their brains with images of the good life (while at the same time practicing a deceptive "tricks and traps" business model according to Harvard Law Professor Elizabeth Warren, also head of the TARP Oversight Committee), electronics retailers teasing them with images of home theaters with 55-inch flat-screen TVs and cell phones that do everything but breathe, companies like Ameriprise telling them that retirement will be life on the beach with exotic islands and catamarans. *Where does it all end?* Eventually, they begin to think they actually *NEED* all these things, not to mention a 3,500-square-foot center hall colonial with a beamed family room/dining room/kitchen, to succeed on their journey. Yet their funds are limited. They can't keep up. So, perhaps, they start taking on credit card debt. Soon it gets out of control. One month they look at their credit card statement (or, more appropriately, statements) and *OUUUCCCHHHHHHH!!!*

So when the Wizard seduces them with the allure of cash back refinancing at a low variable rate, it's like shooting fish in a barrel. They sign on the dotted line.

Can we blame them? Perhaps, but the same business community that tried so hard to push all these goods and services down their throats, financed by their too-good-to-be-true credit terms, have at the same time been robbing our Boomers blind in the workplace.

How, you ask?

Since 1979, overall income in the U.S. has risen 27%. Not so bad on the surface, but, unfortunately, a full one-third of that increase went to the top 1% of wage earners. The bottom 60% of wage earners actually make less today (95 cents on the dollar as of 2004) than they did in 1979. Those between the 60th and 80th percentiles, probably representative of our Boomer couple, earn $1.02 versus 1979 compared to the top 5%, which earns $1.53![5]

It gets even worse when you look at the compensation levels of CEOs. In 1960 the average CEO earned 42 times more than a factory worker. In

2004, that figure rose to 411 times the income of an average factory worker. *Spare us, please: Is anyone really worth that much of a premium, particularly considering the performance of most American corporations over the last several years?* With all this income inequality rampant, it's no wonder that the top 1% of U.S. wealth holders held 42% of total U.S. financial wealth (not including home equity) while the bottom 80% held only 8%![6]

Why is all of this important? As our Baby Boomers have strived to progress through life, less money has gone to them, and more and more money has gone to the wealthy, including those overpaid CEOs; and according to the Philippon and Rhesef study cited earlier, much of this outrageous income disparity, particularly in the finance sector, may not have been completely justified.

So can you really blame our Boomer couple for saying "to hell with it," allowing themselves to be seduced by the promises of the Wizard?

Co-starring:

The Clinton Administration/Fannie Mae/Freddie Mac (as modern-day Mr. Smith, Fannie and Freddie). In 1999 the Clinton Administration pushed Fannie Mae to expand mortgage loans to lower income people, particularly minorities and low-income consumers. This resulted in a program that allowed borrowers who hadn't previously qualified for a Fannie Mae-backed loan to obtain a conventional 30-year loan at a 1 percentage point premium to their more creditworthy neighbors. If they made their monthly payments on time for two years, the 1 point premium would be removed.[7] *So what did this really mean?* It meant that Fannie Mae would now purchase mortgages that had previously been considered sub-prime from banks and other institutions. Previously, these types of loans, granted to less creditworthy customers, were restricted to finance companies that would charge a 3 to 4 point premium.

Concurrently, as Clinton was moving his administration to the center, he signed several pieces of legislation pushed by then Senator Phil

Gramm of Texas. A flamboyant free-market advocate, Gramm sponsored the Gramm-Leach-Bliley Act, which would allow the combination of investment and commercial banks – effectively repealing major parts of the Glass-Steagall Act of 1933, which specifically separated these entities due to the abuses of the 1920s. Then, in the final days of the Clinton Administration, Gramm pushed through legislation that would effectively block future regulation of the markets for derivatives and swaps.[8] And what does the ex-Senator Gramm do today? He's an investment banker/lobbyist for UBS.

Who woulda thunk?

The Bush Administration (as the New Sheriff in Town and his Sidekick). When George W. Bush entered office, he inherited a budget surplus of $128 billion, following three consecutive surpluses of $69 billion, $126 billion and $236 billion (Source: Congressional Budget Office). At that time, the Clinton Administration was projecting a $1.9 trillion surplus over the next 10 years (obviously, this was before 9/11, the Iraq and Afghanistan wars and the Bush tax cuts). One of the key issues of the presidential race in 2000 was what to do with this projected $1.9 trillion. Al Gore proposed a "modest" pro-working family tax cut of $500 billion while using the balance to pay down the national debt (a consequence of which would be to help interest rates stay relatively low), put Social Security in a veritable "lock box" and provide more funding for Medicare. Bush proposed a much more prodigious tax cut of $1.3 trillion, stating that "my plan sets out to make life better for average men, women and children."[9]

But did it?

According to a study by the Congressional Budget Office, the very rich were the prime beneficiaries of the Bush tax cuts. In 2004 the average effective tax rate of middle-income families—those earning an average of $56,200—dropped from 5% in 2000 to 2.9%. Contrastingly, the average effective tax rate for the top 1% of U.S. families—those earning an average of $1.25 million—dropped from 24.2% in 2000 to 19.6% in 2004, a decrease of 4.6 points—more than double the decrease than their middle income counterparts. Interestingly, the average tax cut for this top 1% of income earners amounted to $58,000 per family, *in excess of the middle class taxpayers entire income!*[10]

Proponents of the Bush tax cuts could argue that the rich pay the most taxes and, therefore, should get the most relief. Indeed, according to the same Congressional Budget Office study, the top 1% of households paid 36.7% of federal income taxes. So what's wrong with that? Well, the top 1% control 42% of U.S. financial wealth (this measure excludes housing). Yes, *wealth,* not income. *So isn't this apples and oranges, comparing income to wealth?* Not at all, high income abetted by lower taxes translates into savings that build wealth over time, which is a good thing if wealth is distributed equitably. But our middle-income families, despite much lower tax rates and share of taxes paid, in most cases *can't save at all*—or worse yet, are forced to take on debt just to get by. So while their rich counterparts are saving more, and ultimately increasing the disparity of wealth in America, our middle-class families are slipping further behind. Based on these figures, you can make the argument that the *very rich are not paying enough taxes!*

So what does this have to do with our Baby Boomers who were busted by the downturn of 2008/2009? A lot. First of all, it enabled the atmosphere of greed to accelerate—as the rich get richer, do you think they get satisfied? *Of course not.* The more they get, the more they want—that's simple human nature. So they create more exotic instruments like CDOs and CDSs with higher potential yields. Second, would you like to take odds on how many of that top 1%, those getting the lion's share of the tax cut, were the exact same people who were creating the mess we're now in, wreaking havoc on the U.S. economy and housing market and bringing down companies like Bear Stearns, Lehman Brothers, AIG, Merrill Lynch, General Motors and Chrysler? Third, those tax dollars could have been alternatively used to buttress the Social Security Trust and fund Medicare and other programs that directly benefit our middle-class Baby Boomers. Last, the excess discretionary income in the hands of the very wealthy allows them to bid up the prices of goods and services—particularly housing—making it even harder for our middle-class Boomers to make ends meet.

So how can George W. Bush ever argue that his tax cuts made "life better for average men, women and children"?

What's more, Bush and his cronies weren't big fans of regulation, either.

Hank Paulson (as the Carpetbagger). When things got out of control, Treasury Secretary Hank Paulson, along with his sidekick Federal Reserve Chairman Ben Bernanke went to Congress to ask for the $700+ billion TARP bailout. In effect they had no choice. Without government intervention, we could have all been funneled into an economic death spiral. But isn't it interesting—and great fodder for a story of cinematic proportions—that one of the leaders of Wall Street, who as CEO of Goldman Sachs presided over the initiation of billions of dollars of CDOs, used government money—*our money*—to bail out his old cronies and even his former firm?

And Introducing:

China (as the rich ingénue). As a result of its phenomenal growth, China holds the world's largest reserve of foreign exchange, about $2 trillion. $1 trillion of this reserve is invested in U.S. Treasuries, giving the U.S. a willing lender to finance its budget deficits. However, will China continue to be our lender of choice in the future? As recently as March 2009, Premier Wen Jiabao expressed concerns about his country's investment in the U.S.[11] It's sort of a double-edged sword, though: The more we borrow, the riskier our debt, which is bad for the Chinese. Yet this very same borrowing finances the growth that creates American demand for Chinese goods, allowing China to achieve huge trade surpluses and accumulate more reserves to buy more of our debt.

What a tangled web we weave!

And the Upcoming Sequel: "Great Expectations." Can Barack Obama and his new administration pull us out of this mess and save our Baby Boomers from devastation? Will our Boomer couple be able to keep their home and achieve their retirement dreams? Will the world as we know it ever be the same again?

Coming to Theaters September 2012…or thereabouts.

There it is: the story of our demise. Too many players. Too many plots and subplots. Too little responsibility. Way too little regulation. Way too many resources and too much power concentrated in the hands of way too few.

But, ultimately, it was greed that caused the downturn; growing rapidly in the Petri dish of a laissez-faire business environment thanks to Phil Gramm and his free-market advocates, abetted by the Bush tax cuts, enabled by the Clinton Administration's liberalized housing policies and Fannie Mae and Freddie Mac, hawked on the street by hucksters like Mozilo and Countrywide, and sliced and diced by Wall Street into parasitic toxic monsters that would eventually feed on their very makers, only to be bailed out by Hank Paulson, one of Wall Street's own, with wheelbarrows full of taxpayers' dollars and even more government debt that would hopefully be bought up by the Chinese.

In a convoluted nutshell, that's how the generation of promise became the generation of panic.

* * *

Chapter 3

Birds of a Feather

In Chapter 1, I examined Baby Boomers' attitudes, behaviors, consumption patterns, stress levels and a bevy of other factors and how they've changed due to the impact of the economic downturn. I painted with broad brushstrokes and uncovered some interesting insights. But now let's focus even more precisely.

As I analyzed the responses from our Boomers, we found that they fell into five different groups, or *segments* as those in the marketing community refer to them, each with a somewhat different pattern of responses to the questions we asked.

So here are our Boomer segments:
- **Angry Affluent Progressives**
- **Angry Affluent Traditionals**
- **Mad Moderate Middlers**
- **Stressed and Strained**
- **The Untrusting**

But first, the Similarities Within Our Differences

I would be remiss in overstating the differences among these groups without first noting that they share many things in common. They're all about the same age; they've all cut back on consumption to some degree or another; they've all cut back on credit card usage; they're all angry at business and government institutions; most have seen their socioeconomic status knocked down a rung or two; and they're all feeling a certain degree of stress and anxiety.

What really separates our segments is *their degree of response* in each of these areas. So let's begin.

Segment #1: Angry Affluent Progressives. This group claimed the highest income and net worth among all of our segments and expressed the least decrease in consumption of goods and services, including vacations, meals out at restaurants and leisure activities. Predictably, they also claimed the highest socioeconomic status both pre- and post-downturn, albeit not without a degree of caution: "Don't know how much longer 'Okay' will last," one of them mentioned. They appear to be "real estate rich" insofar as they claimed the largest home value declines among all of our segments and also expressed a high dependence on the sale of their existing residence to fund their retirements.

Our Angry Affluent Progressives (AAPs) are also concerned about funding higher education for their children. "My child will go to college, but I'll be applying for more financial aid than originally intended," one of them told us. Another stated, "Although we have saved for college, the fund is drastically depleted. Options for schools may have to change."

Due to the uncertainty of their home value and, in many cases, the need to fund their children's higher education with depleted resources, they expressed a high level of doubt as to whether they will be able to retire comfortably.

"I have enough to live on," one of our AAPs told us, "but not to retire in the way I thought I would. So I'll be 'fine' but not as 'fine' as I expected unless the stock market picks up."

And another: "But retirement will be very late in life."

They are most sympathetic to the Clinton and Obama administrations, expressing positive feelings toward both, and place slightly above average blame on the Bush Administration. Otherwise, they are pretty much angry at business and government institutions across the board.

One of them expressed what appeared to be a common theme: "The effects of 'capitalism' as we have known it over the last two decades has demonstrated that when left to his own devices, man will choose greed over good. There absolutely has to be regulation.'

"Progressive" they may be, but they're not without a certain degree of old-fashioned capitalism running through their veins as well. "I think the government should provide equal access to health and education. Beyond that, let the market reward the hardworking and innovative when it comes to housing and retirement."

Upscale and progressive with a tinge of capitalistic instincts, yet with real concerns about their children's education, the value of their homes and their ability to retire comfortably, define our AAPs.

Then, of course, there's always the exception to the rule.

"I have enough money to weather any storm," one of the most well-to-do of the group proclaimed.

Segment #2: Angry Affluent Traditionals. This group is similar to the AAPs, but they have a bit more confidence in their abilities to weather the economic storm and they rely more on traditional values. Although Angry Affluent Traditionals (AATs) claim to have cut back less on consumption than most of the other segments (except for the AAPs), they seem to have always been thrifty to the core, downturn or not.

"We already live within our means."

"I've always spent conservatively."

"Didn't spend on things that were just nice to have."

Their already-inherent sense of thriftiness was only exacerbated due to the downturn.

"No more traditional family vacations."

"I have the recession in the back of my mind as I shop and plan vacations, etc."

"All non-essential expenses were reduced significantly or eliminated."

This group experiences less stress than the average Boomer and is more confident in their ability to retire, although not without reservations:

"I THOUGHT I was entering pre-retirement, but I've watched my savings evaporate, still need to work."

Our AATs exhibit an interesting pattern in terms of who they cast blame on for the downturn, slinging slightly less at the Bush Administration and, unlike their more progressive counterparts, casting slightly more responsibility on the Clinton and Obama Administrations and, of course, the Democratic Congress.

"The Clintons set the stage with the lenders being forced to give people mortgages who obviously could not afford them. Obama wasn't in office when the stage was set but I don't see him doing anything at all to help the situation in a clear and realistic manner. We are doomed."

"How about our members in congress and the senate. VERY RESPONSIBLE!!!"

Most of all, this group personifies tradition. Among all the segments, they notched the highest level of response to "I plan to work 'til I drop because I want to," indicating allegiance to that Protestant work ethic we hear so much about. One of the AATs expressed his disdain for the large multinational financial institutions by stating, "Small banks that stuck to the tried and true are fine today." Sort of a Jimmy Stewart/ George Bailey/Frank Capra view of life.

Despite their tendency toward more Republican values, this group certainly doesn't give the Bush Administration a pass and actually expresses positive feelings towards the new Obama Administration:

"The Bush Administration sunk this country due to lack of regulation. Obama will pull it out."

Segment #3: Mad Moderate Middlers. On almost all factors, this group—our 3Ms—are straight down the middle, expressing the "average" response of our entire group of respondents. They've cut back on consumption of everyday products, they're deferring or putting off most of their durable goods purchases, they're planning on using credit cards less in the future and they're unsure about their retirement:

"One income earner left…struggling with three children, mortgage, college tuition, etc."

"Stopped contributing to 401K for fear of losing it."

"As a Texas teacher, my retirement pension will be appx. $3900 per month before taxes and medical insurance. Retirement becomes a joke."

"Cut back on non-essential media costs (Netflix) and look at coupons/ discounts for everyday products."

"Postponed some major purchases including a new car. Looking into refinancing. Cut back on dining out."

"My goal is to eliminate all credit card debt and to avoid any future credit card use that is not absolutely necessary."

"I avoid a balance (on my credit cards), but their fees are horrible so I avoid them even more now."

"The key here is DEBT. Never borrow on cards, but do use heavily as transaction tools."

In terms of casting blame for the downturn, the 3Ms direct most of their angst toward the usual suspects—mortgage companies, Wall Street, investment bankers, hedge fund managers, large multinational banks and the Bush Administration— and are slightly forgiving of the Clinton and Obama Administrations, but not Congress:

"You left out congress which I would put as the number one cause of the problem."

"What about Congress and their requirements for housing for all?"

"Someone gave the homeowners loans on the houses they couldn't afford."

"When we applied for a mortgage, we were interrogated. If banks had stuck to that type of qualification process, we wouldn't be in this mess."

One Boomer, however, nominated a new culprit for our current predicament—our parents' generation:

"As a 'Boomer' I am becoming increasingly sensitive to the media's portrayal of our generation as a growing economic burden. The numeric size of the 'Baby Boomers' has been transparent from its conception (pun intended). Unfortunately, the generation that preceded us either ignored the impact of the huge population increase, or they lacked the vision to institute policies that may have lessened the effects of the aging 'Boomer' population."

Segment 4: Stressed and Strained. Among all the candidly robust comments we received from this group, one stood out as emblematic, if not thoroughly representative, of their feelings:

"I have no retirement plan. We have little savings and that's it. I will work until I can't and then die."

While morbid, the comment reflects, and admittedly, exaggerates, the overall doom and gloom mentality of this group—the S-Squareds, as I like to call them. They're cutting back significantly more on their consumption activities, particularly nonessentials such as vacations, leisure activities and wardrobe:

"Bought a very less than gas guzzling car. Stopped going out to eat as much. Kept my golf clubs in the garage, etc."

"Had just closed my company, looking for a job, then September (happened). Living off savings and equity. Cutting back on everything. To some (this is a) recession, to others much more."

"I think about purchases a lot more now, which is not altogether bad. More people need to learn that lesson and maybe that's one good thing about this recession, it's taught people to think about where they spend their money."

They report the lowest income, the lowest net-worth and low perceived socioeconomic status both pre- and post-downturn.

"Lost 75% of my net worth during the tech bubble. Now this."

"Spouse was laid off, so things are tighter."

"Tough times, but the show must go on."

Without doubt, the downturn has affected some of their most cherished plans. One of our Boomers was quite explicit as to how the downturn has slung a fierce double-whammy at her family.

"Our biggest current worry is the complete drop in the college funds value at the worst possible time. We need the money this year and the next five years. This sadly will affect which colleges my children can attend. Our biggest future worry is our retirement funds have dropped 35% in value. I always thought I'd want to work some in retirement, but I dread it being a NECESSITY."

The key defining characteristic of our S-Squareds is the overall stress and anxiety the downturn has thrust into their lives. By far, they were the most stressed-out group of the bunch.

"I always worry about my job."

"Sometimes I just can't believe we are here."

"I definitely feel more stressed about my retirement savings. I'm hoping I won't have to work until I'm 80."

"Fear of the unknown, and I don't know who to blame."

Like their peers in the other groups, S-Squareds are upset at government and business and aren't shy to tell us about it:

"Companies need regulation and oversight and this recession proves it."

"This country (and the world) needed a wake-up call. We were out of control with consumption. At the rate we were going there was no way to continue to support an economy like that, something had to give. We needed to create a stable foundation and rebuild with industries we can continue to support, like renewable energy, alternative fuel cars, organic family farms and public transportation. I hope that if one lesson was learned from all this it's that we need to think about what we buy and why."

Although painful, ironically, the effects of the downturn may have been enlightening and a source of hope that the future can be different and better.

"I was always a big believer that the market would be the driving force in keeping companies honest, but clearly this is not the case. Senior management at companies have been rewarded whether they succeeded in building VALUE or not. Short-term stock fluctuations were manipulated to show value that wasn't real. So I feel the companies' executives and boards cannot be trusted to create real long-term value without intervention, sadly."

"Again, I have not been panicking yet. There's some feeling that we're all in the same boat and it will all work out. But I do tend to be an optimist."

"Eventually things will get back to a NEW normal."

Segment #5: The Untrusting. Perhaps our most interesting group is The Untrusting, which although all over the political spectrum, are characterized by their *complete distrust of everyone*—government, business, liberals, conservatives; they give no one a free pass. Although every other group was somewhat forgiving of the Clinton and Obama Administrations, this group was not.

"The media is saying it is the end of the world and Obama is using this to implement the government takeover of the financial system and healthcare, which will lead us to disaster if not stopped."

Their political views run the gamut: liberal, conservative, with perhaps a dash of libertarianism, anarchism and rugged individualism thrown in as well:

"We will only get through this if we completely remake Congress and vote all the liberals out over the next four years."

"Abolish the federal reserve!"

"It will take years to regain our former standards of living given leftist rule."

"I believe the downturn was manufactured artificially as a way for some parties to make money and/or as a political tactic. It exploded because of media coverage and the emotional reaction it caused. Disgusting."

"Socialism now and socialism forever."

Overall, this group claims lower incomes and net worths, but it spans a wide range with some of the wealthiest and poorest respondents.

"I am sick of demonizing Wall Street and people like us who have huge mortgages. The bank was telling us we could take out more and we thought, 'They will give us a noose to hang ourselves,' but we still didn't understand the liability completely. We planned on paying down our mortgage in chunks. I do think there was Wall Street and banking greed, but not everyone. Don't demonize all of Wall Street."

"My personal economic downturn began in December 2001, post-9/11, and never rebounded."

"Retirement will come and we will have to make serious changes in lifestyle."

"Have sufficient wealth to retire comfortably."

For most of them, the downturn has affected their daily lives and has spurred them to make changes in their daily routines, some of which are quite dramatic.

"Only buy groceries on sale, one bottle of wine a week, plan all errands carefully to save on gas, no new clothing for a long time."

"I stopped shopping. That was a personal decision. I took a hard look at where our money was going after I started doing all the financials in our house. Knowledge is power. I also got a job in an effort to take responsibility for my personal debt."

"My husband lost his job, no thanks to the Ponzi scheme by Allen Stanford. We are using savings and getting help from family. We are also looking to refinance our mortgage, which is too big."

"We are already behind two months on the rent but our landlord is very understanding."

"Cut back on all superfluous spending and declared bankruptcy."

Individuals to the core, they're distrustful of Social Security (government distrust) and their 401Ks (business distrust) as well as the sale of their existing residences (real estate and banking industry distrust) to fund their retirements. They're a very disillusioned group—or perhaps not:

"I can't say I am disillusioned because I already knew this was how it was (I had a dismal view to begin with). I think it is a lousy time to be trying to survive economically but I think it is a good thing because we needed to level the playing field. It's like a wildfire—devastating but necessary to future growth and health."

Finally, there was one short but sweet statement that I thought epitomized the collective character of this group to a tee:

"I'm mad as hell, but have no choice whether to take it or not."

Five different groups, five different perspectives.

The *Angry Affluent Progressives* with their liberal bias, real estate wealth and higher income.

The *Angry Affluent Traditionals* with their self-confidence, their Protestant work ethic and their inherent thrifty nature.

The *Mad Moderate Middlers,* reflecting a straight-down-the-middle perspective on the current circumstances.

The *Stressed and Strained,* worrisome to the core, and boxed in by economic constraints that they cannot control.

The Untrusting, mad as hell, and trusting of no one.

Five different variations on a theme, yet many similarities: They've all been affected by the downturn in some way, they're all angry at our business and government institutions and most of them have had to seriously adjust their consumption patterns and plans for retirement.

But let's sharpen our focus even more.

Let's examine how the downturn has impacted the lives of eight individuals and families, each with a unique and different story to tell.

* * *

PART II

Left in Its Wake...

Chapter 4

Empty Bucket

Dick Shaughnessy's current predicament is as a direct result of the forces that caused the economic meltdown. He worked for a small company that got acquired and merged three times until he became part of Citigroup, one of those companies deemed 'too big to fail.' As a result of the repeal of the Glass-Steagall Act, Citigroup was allowed to branch out into riskier practices, which ultimately cost Shaughnessy his job and most of his 401K.

* * *

"I had this sort of bucket list in my head," 55-year-old Brooklyn native Dick Shaughnessy told me, "everything I'd like to do once in my life before I'm gone, you know, like see the major sporting events—things like the Kentucky Derby, the NCAA Final Four, the Super Bowl. Beyond that, my goals for retirement were relatively modest. I figured I'd look forward to having the time for visiting friends and family around the country. We were considering buying a place in Florida to live the snowbird lifestyle, commuting back and forth from New York. I had hoped my savings would provide an annual interest that I could live off."

"So when did you think you'd be able to do all these things?" I asked.

"A year ago, I thought I was in a good position to retire soon," he answered. "Not that anything was imminent, but the numbers were looking good, I was getting close. Then the walls came tumbling down."

And tumble down they did.

Dick Shaughnessy had worked in telecommunications for Citigroup—one of those *too big to fail* mega-financial institutions—for 11 years. Half of his 401K was in Citigroup stock. Before the crash, the stock was worth more than $50 per share. During the crash, it nosedived to as low as $2. As of this writing, it's at about $5. *Ouch!*

"So you do the math," Shaughnessy continued, "the half of my 401K that was in Citigroup stock went down by close to 95%. The other half was in a portfolio of stocks that pretty much mirrored the market. That was down by 30% or 40%. So what's the average, down about 60%?"

Having his 401K tumble by almost 60% is painful enough, but to add insult to injury, Shaughnessy was laid off in late 2008. "In many ways, it's not the most terrible thing in the world. The guys left in my department are being worked to the bone."

A down-to-earth, meat-and-potatoes guy, Shaughnessy grew up in a part of Brooklyn that's permanently stuck in a 1960s and 1970s time warp; he even admits that once or twice he frequented *2001*, the Brooklyn disco immortalized in the film *Saturday Night Fever*. A Mets fan, his musical tastes run the gamut from Frankie Valli and the Four Seasons and Connie Francis to Country Joe and the Fish. Although intrigued by the concept of *The Sopranos*, he refused to watch the show during its heyday, because, "there's still a few of those type guys around here and I don't find that lifestyle very entertaining."

In his youth, Shaughnessy never planned to work in telecommunications or on Wall Street or in financial services for that matter. His dream was to be a teacher. "I went to college and majored in elementary education. Then I went on to get my Masters. Of course, I wanted to stay in the city. But in 1975 and 1976 there was a freeze on hiring. They hadn't fired a teacher in years in New York City, so employment-wise, I was caught in a sort of gridlock. You couldn't get on a list, you couldn't take a test. Nothing. So, not only was I not able to pursue the career I desired, I had to start looking for work in other areas."

Luckily, his father came to the rescue. "My dad had worked for New York Telephone for 45 years. Like a good father, one day he came home and said, 'Here's an application, fill it out.' About a year later, I got called in for a job."

Shaughnessy began in New York Telephone's customer service department. But when the federal court busted up Ma Bell in 1983, Shaughnessy moved into sales and marketing at American Bell, the subsidiary that sold equipment. Then he was transferred to business services at AT&T Network Services.

After 10 years, Shaughnessy left AT&T and began working as a consultant for a small brokerage house on Wall Street. "I did it for about five years," Shaughnessy recalls. "I kind of liked it. It was a small firm and I was their 'everything guy.' In addition to handling telecommunications, I also did PC stuff, software stuff, everything. It was a refreshing break from working for a big company."

Unfortunately, this refreshing break came to an end in 1998. "The firm began to have trouble and started cutting back. I was given the old warning that I would be among the first to go should they have to make another round of cutbacks. So I put my resume out on the street and got a position at another banking/brokerage house called Schroders. Now I was working in telecommunications at a medium-sized firm, but in a small department."

Yet through no fault of his own, Shaughnessy soon found himself working for a large corporation once again. As a consequence of the 1999 repeal of the Glass-Steagall Act, which formerly disallowed the combination of commercial banks and investment banks, merger mania hit the financial services arena. So Schroders got bought by Salomon Brothers, which was still finalizing its merger with Smith Barney, which was then bought by Citigroup.

"In two short years, by not doing a thing, I worked for three different companies," Shaugnessy quipped.

Without doubt, this shuffling from company to company was not an enjoyable experience for Shaughnessy. "I can understand that when one firm gets bought by another, that the top execs at the buying firm hold all the cards. But I was shocked to see that it was the same way in the trenches. Even at the lowest levels, the same things were taking place. My colleagues and I just got thrown around. It wasn't very pleasurable.

"Citigroup officially took over in Spring 2001. Early that summer, one of my jobs was closing out the old headquarters. I was literally the last guy out. Near the end of the summer, I reported to my new office in Tribeca. I went from working in uptown or midtown to downtown. And, of course, we all know what happened next."

On the morning of September 11, 2001, Dick Shaughnessy reported to work at the company's huge headquarters building in Tribecca at about eight o'clock. When the first strike hit, a little bit of buzz circulated through the office. "We were all sitting at our cubicles," said Shaughnessy. "In our world of telecom, when something goes wrong, the system can go down, you can have a power outage. We were all asking, 'What's going on?' Then someone says, 'A plane hit the Trade Center.' Of course, at that point, we all thought it was a commuter plane. One of the supervisors had a TV monitor in his office.

We all crowded around. The first pictures of the tower were pretty dark. You couldn't see much, but we still thought it was some sort of accident. Then we watched live as the second plane hit. The instant that happened, our supervisor said, '*Two planes is not an accident. Clear this place out now!*'

"We rushed out of the building onto Greenwich Street. If you look up the street, it's a direct shot to the Trade Center. If you remember that day, the sky was perfectly blue, not a cloud to be seen. It was a sight that I'll always remember—the burning towers, black billowing smoke, yellow and orange flames, against that bright blue sky. Then a woman from across the street started shouting, 'They've just attacked the pentagon!' Then I remember a cop, I think, said 'You've got to get out of here, start walking north!' I figured I'd have to walk home. So I called my wife, assured her I was okay and told her to meet me at this restaurant we knew across the Williamsburg Bridge. As I walked north toward Greenwich Village, I remember seeing people huddled around this truck driver who had a radio. Someone said, 'There's people jumping out the towers.' I thought for a moment about looking back, but I just couldn't. It was about as horrible a thing as I could imagine and I just couldn't look back. Then someone yelled, 'The tower's collapsed!' Never in my wildest imagination would I have thought that the World Trade Center would collapse. I looked back and saw all the smoke. Then when I got up to around Houston Street, the other collapsed. Finally, after several hours, I crossed the Williamsburg Bridge and met my wife at the restaurant. The restaurant had a small bar with a great view of the city. I remember there was a TV set hanging overhead. Of course, it was focused on the smoke and destruction. My eyes were glued to it. Then I looked out the window toward lower Manhattan and saw the exact same thing—the smoke, the fire, the devastation, the destruction. I'll tell you, that was probably the most surreal experience of my life."

Shaughnessy told me about the most poignant moment of his day, a moment that took place right before he crossed the bridge. "I thought for a moment about buying a disposable camera. I thought even though this is horrible, it's historical, so maybe I should snap a few pictures. I looked back at the black smoke, paused, and shook my head. No, I said to myself, this is way too sacred, this is not to be trifled with. Then I walked over the bridge."

In the blurry wave of emotions flying through his nerves at the time, he thought about the safety of two people very close to him. "My brother was a commodities trader who worked in one of the towers. I found out he wasn't going in until nine-thirty that day. He was safe. One of my closest childhood friends worked as a bond trader on the 105th floor." He paused for a moment. "We lost him."

9/11 was not the only key Baby Boomer event that impacted Shaughnessy's life. Like many Boomers, he was affected by most of the key epochal events of the time, including Vietnam, Watergate and Woodstock.

"I sort of stumbled onto Woodstock," he told me. "My family had a country house in upstate New York, not too far from the Woodstock festival. Every summer when school let out, we'd pack up all our things in our car—I was the oldest of six kids so it was crowded—and drove out to the country. The big treat was that on Saturdays my parents would take us into town. On the Woodstock weekend, we went into town and we saw hundreds and hundreds of hippies. I was sort of naive and only 16 at the time, and I asked one of them, 'What's going on? The guy looked at me bewildered and said, *'You haven't heard of Woodstock?'* To this day, even though I never set foot on the festival grounds, I love that music and I love that movie."

Today Shaughnessy lives with his wife, an employee with a major airline, in a two-family house in a middle-class Brooklyn neighborhood.

Like most of New York, the neighborhood is a real melting pot. "When I was growing up, this neighborhood was all Irish and Italian. Nearby, you had another area that was primarily Scandanavian. Now it's all different. You still have a big chunk of Irish and Italians, but in a slightly smaller area. But then on the outskirts you have every other nationality you can think of—Spanish, Indians, Chinese, Koreans, Russians, everything."

As he sat on his front porch, he told me about when he first heard rumblings of the downturn.

"Probably when I got laid off, in October 2008," he answered. "That's when I first heard of it. It was really a shock. Citigroup had historically not laid off many people. And, then, a whole group of us got let go all at once."

Initially, Shaughnessy still thought he was in relatively good shape. "My Citigroup stock was still in the 40s back then. So even with a little bit of a hit, my 401K was still fine. The funny thing is there was still time to get out. No one knew the company was going into the crapper. When the news started breaking that the government was going to have to bail out the banks, that's when the stock went off the charts. But there was never anyone around to tell me, 'Get out! It's going to two!'"

So are there any other substantial liquid assets you have to help fund your retirement?

"Just a minimal amount. I have a minimal pension from AT&T and also a minimal one from Citigroup. I've tried, but I can't even find how much they're worth. Not much, though, you can be sure of that."

How about your house?

"That's our saving grace, actually. The house will be completely paid for in two years. Although we don't have substantial liquid assets, we have enough to pay down our mortgage. And since we have no kids, we don't have college costs to worry about. If we did, we'd really be in trouble."

How has the downturn affected your lifestyle?

"The answer is obvious," he said. "We cut back. My wife has a meager salary, but every little bit helps. Ironically, her job's best perk is free travel. Even though airfare is free to us, we haven't traveled since my layoff. We go out less on Saturday nights for dinner, but that's not such a big deal. I got a modest package from Citigroup when they let me go—two weeks for every year and they threw a little extra in, so I got paid for about thirty weeks. All of my colleagues who got let go had to immediately go on COBRA. I was lucky, I was on my wife's health plan."

So here you are, you had a good job and a pretty healthy 401K. Then all of a sudden because of mistakes made by senior management and Wall Street, you get stunned with the double whammy of being laid off and losing most of your life savings. How do you feel about that?

He thought for a moment, then answered, "I feel like I've been ripped off, especially when you see so many people skating from companies with huge bonuses and golden parachutes. But I try not to think about how much my 401K has gone down. There's simply nothing I can do about it. It might be the poker player in me—the last hand is over, start thinking about the next one or you'll get beat."

Then, he paused again. "You know, you have to take everything in context. My financial suffering is a small price to pay compared to some of our friends and relatives who lost their lives on 9/11 or in battles overseas."

In many respects, Dick Shaughnessy's is a Baby Boomer's life in microcosm, subjected to the key events and forces that have shaped all Baby Boomer's lives. He was touched by Vietnam, Woodstock, Watergate and 9/11. His work life was affected by the public breakup of Ma Bell. He was mergered and acquisitioned from company to company until, finally, he found himself working at a company that was "too big to fail." The repeal of the Glass-Steagall Act allowed that company to get into riskier investment practices. Then when the wizards of Wall Street outsmarted themselves, he took the bullet right in the chest.

So what do you think caused the economic meltdown?

"There are a couple of things, though. Going back to that fateful day, 9/11. Aside from the loss of life, I think about what it did to business. It was such a brutal attack, but a year or so later, people thought everything was normal again. I just couldn't understand that. I thought that something that huge can't go away that fast. I had this gut feeling that things just can't be that rosy, that there's still a lot of bad stuff lurking."

You were there, right in the center of the storm, on Wall Street. What did you think about Wall Street's role in the downturn?

"Yeah, well, being in brokerage and banking I saw a lot of stuff. I saw these people, these traders, getting thrown million-dollar bonuses left and right. You know those guys—those guys getting the big bonuses—looked just like you and me. Heck, if we had a cousin that would put us in a trading chair, we could've done the job just as well as them. I'm sure of it. I just don't know if people should be worth tens of millions of dollars. At a certain point, it's got to end. It's just got to."

So what's next for Dick Shaughnessy?

"Well, as I said, a year ago, I thought I'd be able to retire soon. But I didn't have much time to even hold that thought. I guess my bucket list will have to wait. I'll just have to go back to work. I'll have to find a job and work much longer than I ever imagined." He shook his head. "Much longer."

As will many of his fellow Boomers.

* * *

Chapter 5

What Do the Simple Folk Do?

I n a memorable scene from the musical Camelot, Queen Guinevere asks King Arthur what the "simple folk" do to keep themselves occupied. After Arthur recites a litany of activities, she seems startled. He reassures her by saying, "I have it on the best authority." And he certainly did—as the young Wart, presumably of humble origins, Arthur was once one of the "simple folk" himself. He had the unique vantage point to understand their plight from both perspectives. So does Donna Dellasandro.

* * *

Imagine peaceful rolling green pastures, shaded by voluminous rows of sturdy maples, black birches, catalpas bursting with popcorn-white buds and tall white oaks, all fluttering in a restful calming breeze. Imagine great temples built to the Gods of Conspicuous Consumption—a 5,000-square-foot mansion, three and a half bathrooms (all marble and with a sunken tub in the master "suite"), with closets as large as East Village studios, wine cellars, media centers, beamed great rooms, swooping handcrafted staircases, swimming pools and manicured grounds (one even had snow trucked in at Christmastime to enhance the mood). Imagine bleach-blonde housewives tending to their daily chores in their Chevy Suburbans, cell phones dangling from their ears like jewelry as they guzzle gas in delightful glee. Imagine older teens in their chinos, penny loafers and Ralph Lauren shirts, driving to high school in their birthday-present Hummers. Imagine a homogenized, modern-day Rockwellian world, free of crime, pollution, trash, sewage, hunger and pain. *In short, there's simply not a more congenial spot....*

A Camelot for the new aristocracy? you ask.

Perhaps, in a metaphorical sense, but in reality, it's just one of the ultra-wealthy towns in Fairfield County, Connecticut, the *gold coast,* as it's often referred to, home to investment bankers, hedge fund managers, CEOs and other masters of the universe, even some of those notoriously infamous AIG execs who accepted their seven-figure bonuses despite the federal bailout.

But, everything can't be that perfect, you may say. *Even Camelot had its haves and have-nots.*

Correct! I answer. One need not look any further than Donna Dellasandro—at different times in her life, she's lived in both settings.

"I *never, ever, ever* looked at a price in the grocery store before," she told me. "Now I'm struggling just to put food on the table." Petite and full of spunk with olive skin and dark hair, Dellasandro personifies her Brooklyn roots. She's proud, tough, street smart, insightful, agile, and creative. Most of all, she's a survivor.

"I've never been poor in my life and now at the age of 56, I'm poorer than I could ever imagine," she said. "The competition for jobs is fierce, my age is against me, I have no money, my car is repossessed, I am begging my landlady to let me stay in my apartment even though I'm behind on the rent. I went from having two cars, a maid twice a week, traveling around the world, never having to think about money, to having no money and no job. I asked the local social services office for some help and I was told I could go to the food bank in town."

Dellasandro's riches-to-rags story begins in a predominantly Italian-American neighborhood in her native Brooklyn. At 16 she announced to her parents that she desired to become what was then referred to as an airline stewardess; she dreamed of seeing the world, meeting interesting people and having wonderful new experiences. But her parents discouraged her, calling the job a glorified waitress in the sky. "They were old school," Dellasandro explained. "For them it wasn't common for a woman to work. I was discouraged from ever being able to excel at anything. It wasn't their fault, though, it's just the way they were raised."

Upon graduation from high school, then, she took a job on Wall Street, but didn't like it. "I hated it," she said without hesitation, "I didn't like the real world, the 9-to-5 grind, living in Brooklyn, getting on the train, going to the city, being told what to do, everything."

After a year, she decided to go to college, enrolling at a branch of CUNY on Staten Island. There she majored in child psychology and interned at Willowbrook, that infamous asylum exposed by a young Geraldo Rivera for its mistreatment of patients. From there, she took a full-time job at a mental-health facility for children in Brooklyn. "I didn't like that either," she said in her own inimitable sort of way. "All I kept hearing were people's problems. One day, I told myself, 'this is what I went to school for? To hear other people's problems?'"

Then came a major pivot point in her career.

She returned to Wall Street, taking a job as a foreign exchange trader. "Those were the 1980s, the wild days," she told me. "It was all about money. The money was flowing and flowing and flowing. Champagne. Limos. The best restaurants. The best clubs. I shopped at the best stores, never even looking at the price tags. I took clients wherever they wanted to go, never worrying about the tab. It was party time."

While vacationing on Paradise Island, she met a man whom she playfully refers to as, "my future ex-husband," an executive with an offshore bank. "Everything was first class for us," she explained. "We traveled around the world, lived in Switzerland and the Bahamas and had a great life."

Within a year, Donna became pregnant. Having accumulated considerable assets, the two of them settled in that idyllic town on Connecticut's fabled gold coast. Those were the salad days for Dellasandro. "I'd go to the gym, go out to lunch, volunteer in my child's school. Basically, I lived a well-balanced, well-to-do life."

You could say things were almost idyllic, except for….

"I noticed a subtle form of resentment from early on," she recalled. "It was definitely a lily-white, bleach-blonde community. There was this underlying bias against people with slightly darker skin and dark hair. It's funny, but when I used to take my Volkswagen to drop off my daughter at school, no one would talk to me. I think they thought I was the nanny. When I used my husband's Audi, then they would acknowledge me. It wasn't until I hooked up with the local Jewish and Italian people—of course, they were few and far between—that I had any real friends."

Ten years later, Dellasandro and her husband divorced

"At that point, I decided I needed a change," she said, "so I sold everything, packed up and moved to Florida with my nine-year-old daughter, Linda. It kept me busy. I had to buy a house, make new friends, get my daughter into school, all those things."

After three years, though, Dellasandro and Linda were on the move again. "I made a fair degree of financial mistakes during those years, mostly in real estate. I also began to realize that Florida wasn't the greatest place to raise a kid, so I decided to move back north."

Dellasandro thrust herself and her daughter back into the belly of the beast, that same idyllic little town in Fairfield County, although this time as a renter, not one of the landed aristocracy. "I took all the money I had left and bought a business, a franchise, a drama school for kids. At first life was good. I was making good money, raising my daughter on my own, calling all the shots."

Although Donna had been exposed to a robust set of life experiences, two threads have been woven throughout her life since her formative days. "I've always loved the movies, since as long as I can remember. My favorite movie of all time has to be Roberto Bennini's *Life Is Beautiful.* A close second? *One Flew Over the Cuckoo's Nest.* It had so much meaning to me, especially knowing what I knew about asylums. My hobby has always been screenwriting. It's my escape."

And the other thread in Dellasandro's life?

"I'm a child of the 1960s. My influences were the Kennedys, Woodstock, the politics of the time, that sense of freedom, peace-loving and anti-war. We were a whole different species back them." When I asked her political affiliation, she didn't hesitate for a moment. "Absolutely, I'm a Democrat. And I find that very difficult living in a Republican town."

Despite her against-the-grain political leanings, Donna enjoyed her new career in Fairfield County. "Owning that business was a great experience for me. I made good money. I was well respected and became well known in the area. It was more than teaching kids about drama, I was giving them life skills as well, teaching them how to look at people, how to respect their peers, build a sense of confidence."

Three years later, though, the foundation began to crack.

"It was about 2005 or so. The economy started getting shaky. Parents were cutting back. They weren't sending their kids for drama training. I didn't get as many contracts. I contemplated selling the franchise, but I couldn't, so I just had to walk away from it."

And the really scary part?

"For the first time in my life I had no money, absolutely no money."

And the even scarier part?

"As a 56- year-old Baby Boomer, I found it almost impossible to get a job. You know, I go on Craig's List, Jobs.com, Monster.com, all of those sites. The people who respond to me are kids. I told one of them, 'I have pants in my closet older than you are.'"

With no savings and no job, other things in her life began to crumble. Her car got repossessed. She fell behind on her rent. At times she couldn't afford groceries. And to rub salt in the wound, she had become poor in what was otherwise a land of plenty. "Yes, it's difficult living in this town. Particularly since I lived here in a nice-size house when my ex-husband and I had considerable wealth. It's tough to see the wealthy around town flaunt it. If I could get out, I would in a heartbeat. I'd love to move to New York, but I have to find a job first. Although, I have to admit, the one silver lining around this town is you feel relatively safe."

Eventually, she found a low-paying job with the local Red Cross, helping them with their event planning. "I like planning events, it's sort of like producing a play or movie. I'd love to be an event planner in the city, but everybody and their brother is. But working at the Red Cross was difficult for me because many of the wealthier moms in town would volunteer there. Ladies who lunch, I like to call them."

Occasionally, she would supplement her income with jobs that played off her experience as a drama coach, a lover of the cinema and an aspiring screenwriter. "For the last two years, I've taken acting gigs on the side. I've been in four movies, two TV shows, a PBS program. I'm listed on a site called NY Casting and sometimes I'll get calls. Hell, it's extra income."

As we walked down the main thoroughfare in town, amid scores of storefront real estate agencies hawking multimillion dollar McMansions, a bevy of antique shops, art galleries and boutique designer clothing stores, I asked her about her feelings over her current economic plight.

"Well, at first, I thought the economy was all media hype," she told me. "Who knows? Maybe it was wishful thinking. But you kept on hearing *the economy, the economy, the economy*. It became real to me when I tried to find a job after I sold the business. Here I am, intelligent with great experience and I couldn't get a job. Then I came to an epiphany. My competition in the job market were 19- and 20-year-olds. I'm a 56-year-old in a 20-something market."

"Talking about 20-somethings, what about your daughter, isn't she college age?" I asked.

She smiled. "I just took Linda off to college for her freshman year last week. She'll be a dance major. Luckily, her father's taking care of that."

As we crossed the intersection, I counted three BMW 7-series, two Mercedes, a Chevy Suburban, and a Jaguar scouting for the parking places wedged diagonally on both sides of the busy street. I thought it was as good a time as any to ask her about stress.

"*Stress?*" she responded immediately. "I'm surprised I still have hair on my head. I wake up in the middle of the night. I ask myself, 'How am I going to do this? How am I going to do that?' You know, I used to have filet mignon three times a week. Now I wonder how I'm going to put food on the table."

"So look around us," I said. "Look at this quaint little town, with the quaint little boutiques, luxury cars all around us, clean-cut teenagers hanging out on the street. Isn't this town in many ways responsible for your plight? Isn't this the lair of some of those wizards of Wall Street who caused this mess?"

"Yes, I know that," she answered. "And I'm angry about it. Yeah, some of the people who live in town—the hedge fund managers, the investment bankers, the bond salesmen—they helped cause the problem. I can't say I'm friends with any of them, but I do know some of them on an acquaintance level. I'm sure a lot of them lost a lot of money, too. But they're still living in their multimillion dollar homes despite all the pain and suffering they inflicted on everyone else."

"Tell me more," I prodded her.

"It's all about greed," she said. "Greed from the people on Wall Street who had control of things. Greed from the mortgage companies who gave mortgages to everyone, even people who had no money. No down payments on cars. We were given a comfort level that we could handle the debt by the mortgage brokers, the bankers, people whom we trusted, because we thought they knew more than we did. Then, of course, we found out they didn't."

"You seem to be a resilient person, a survivor," I said. "Is there anything you can learn from this, something to help fuel the years ahead?"

"The only thing I can say in a positive way, but it really doesn't make me feel any better or different, is that I share this fate with a lot of people," she answered. "I'm not an oddball. There are lots of people out there. People who had decent jobs, lived comfortably and now for the first time in their lives are poor. If you look behind the counter at Wal-mart, you see a different type of person, a person with a middle-class background who used to have a decent job. You see them working at Starbucks, working as crossing guards at the local schools. It makes me feel like I'm not alone. I also see a trend. I see lots of people helping other people, people who in the past were so consumed with their lives that they didn't have the time. They see things from the other side now. It's a humbling experience. It's taught a lot of people to see beyond their wealth, beyond how other people live. They have to realize that towns like this are not the norm."

We decided to go for a ride in my car. She wanted to show me something in the next town over. As I drove, I asked another question:

"Before this all began. When you were still wealthy and with your husband living in a nice house in town, did you ever think about retirement?"

"Oh sure," she answered quickly. "Absolutely. I kept saying that when I'm 55, I want to retire and travel a little bit, maybe pick up a little job because that's my personality." She paused for a moment and sighed. "But that's gone. All gone."

As we rambled down one of the area's winding roads shaded by a canopy of tall maples and oaks, I asked her the inevitable follow-up: "So what do you think about retirement now?"

"I don't think I'll ever be able to retire," she answered. "I have to take it one day at a time. If I look too far into the future, I'll put myself six feet under. My whole life has changed. I can't shop where I used to shop, can't buy the things I used to buy and I can't go into a grocery store without having a very exact list and sticking to it."

"But you're resilient, a survivor, you must have a plan to get you out of this?" I asked.

"Of course. I call it my economic rehab plan," she giggled. "I had to quit the job at the Red Cross. I couldn't make it on that salary, I couldn't pay the rent. With Linda in college, I lost my child support. I couldn't find a job in New York, so I stumbled into one around here."

Really? A new job, a new beginning for Donna Dellasandro?

"I'm going to be doing something I never ever dreamed of doing," she answered teasingly.

So tell me? What is it?

She held her finger up and then motioned for me to make a left turn. We drove down a beautiful street with large homes and flowing green lawns. She signaled for me to stop and then pointed at one of the houses.

"Starting tomorrow, I'm going to be a nanny in that house," she told me with pride and dignity. "The father's a hedge fund manager, can you believe that?" She giggled. "It's a good job, what I need right now, but when I took it, I told myself, *'Oh My God, I had a nanny for my daughter growing up and now I'm a nanny myself.'*"

Reflectively, she took a deep, courageous breath, then mused, "That's the difference between where I came from and where I am right now."

* * *

Chapter 6

Shattered Dreams

A *high-level marketing exec for a major corporation by day, virtually* *penniless at night—how can someone who appears successful to the* *outside world be in such dismal economic straits? Kurt Simpson's story is* *one of long hiatuses between jobs. He depleted his 401K and spent beyond* *his family's means and then to top it off suffered the economic consequences* *of divorce.*

* * *

If one were an interloper at Kurt Simpson's workplace, he or she would undoubtedly observe a talented, good-looking, mid-50ish corporate marketing executive, dressed business casual, competently navigating through the various meetings, conference calls, hallway conversations and reviews of Powerpoint presentations and Excel spreadsheets that occupy most hours of senior-middle-level corporate executives. It wouldn't surprise you to learn he earns a base salary in the mid-100s, with a generous bonus most years.

He's run sales for an in-house marketing group for one of America's most prestigious companies, worked on highly targeted marketing communications campaigns in agribusiness for big companies and at big advertising agencies, headed up marketing for a leading financial services firm and directed the advertising programs for a start-up healthcare company owned by a wealthy entrepreneur.

Undoubtedly, this is a resume of a highly successful person.

So what's wrong with this picture?

"I'm driving a 2000 Volvo with a hundred thousand miles on it. I'm wearing clothes I bought seven years ago. I haven't bought a new pair of shoes in five years. I could barely afford a small two-bedroom apartment," Simpson laments. "Somehow, someway everything slipped through our fingers without us ever realizing it."

Simpson's story begins in a small Midwestern town, a railroad watering depot, halfway between Chicago and Kansas City, the town of his childhood.

In many ways mythical, the town's main thoroughfare – its buildings sprouting like towering mountains out of the windswept plains - is emblematic of all small town Main Streets. There's a quaintness to it, an everybody-knows-everybody sort of folksiness, a sense of security and nurturance. People feel safe here—yeah, the outside world and all its complexities hovers in the rarefied air above, but it never really impacts them, only existing as images on a TV screen or newspaper page. Somehow, someway, the townsfolk are comfortably insulated.

The shops lining Main Street aren't just shops—they're people; they're Sam's pharmacy, soda fountain and all. Mr. Atkinson's movie theater, one screen only. Art's general store—your credit's always good here, neighbor. Gus's hardware emporium—tools, materials and all the advice you would ever need. Floyd's barbershop, its striped pole swirling incessantly, just like the gossip inside. Everyone knows the police chief and his deputy on a first-name basis. The town drunk is more character than criminal.

Mayberry? Disneyland?

A little bit of both, perhaps.

"It was the kind of town," explains Simpson, "where you could run out of your house on a Saturday morning, go get your buddy and not come back until sundown. Parents never worried about safety. The town was like one giant playground. Everybody knew everybody. There was absolutely no crime."

Baby Boomer to the core, Simpson explains that his town provided the community with a protective cover from some of the more radical elements most Boomers associate with their youth. "We were aware of those things, but growing up in a small town, we were insulated. Kids there just didn't do drugs. If you were a hippie, that was no good. Of course, we knew about hippies and Woodstock and all that, but we weren't as worldly as kids are today."

Not surprisingly, it was in his hometown where Simpson first dreamed about what he wanted to do with his life. "Probably when I was a sophomore or junior in high school, I decided I wanted to go into advertising. Maybe I was influenced by Darrin Stevens in *Bewitched,* one of my favorite TV programs, but I was always the creative type. I wrote for the school newspaper and I was the guy everyone came to for ideas for the prom theme, float themes, all that stuff. So I thought it would be nice to make a living doing that, being creative."

When Kurt arrived at college his freshman year, "I registered for journalism and never looked back." Four years later, he graduated with a Bachelor of Journalism in Advertising. His first big career break came when he was working selling ad space for a big Midwestern newspaper in 1975.

"My friend and I were visiting one of our favorite college professors and he told us he had just received a call from an executive at Monsanto and that they were looking for an advertising person in St. Louis. My friend didn't want to relocate. But I shrugged my shoulders and said, 'Why not?'"

Two days later, Simpson received a call from a woman at Monsanto. Two weeks later, he was living in St. Louis.

"I think my guardian angel was with me that day," he recalled. "In many ways landing the job was pure luck. In my interview, she asked me if I knew anything about agriculture. I said, yeah, I used to work in the hay fields back home. She said, 'Perfect match.' The opening was for managing the advertising programs for some of their agricultural products."

St. Louis, the city known for its towering arch—The Gateway to the West—also proved to be the gateway to Simpson's career and adult life for that matter. The small-town kid was now working in one of America's biggest cities for one of America's biggest companies. "It was a plum job," he explained. "Here I am at this Fortune 100 company and they give me a few products and a $7 million budget and say, here, go market them. I got to fly into New York City and go to Madison Avenue to meet with big advertising agencies. It was everything I ever dreamed of."

It was also in St. Louis where Simpson met interior designer Ann McCarthy. "From the very beginning we were best friends, soul mates. We were so secure in our relationship that neither of us cared if one went off for a week with our friends. There was never anything to worry about. We were totally devoted to each other."

Shortly, thereafter Simpson and McCarthy married.

After four and a half years of cutting his teeth at Monsanto, Simpson learned of an opening at a fairly large advertising agency on the West Coast. "At that point, we were truly living a dream, living in a major metro area and me working for a big agency in town on a fairly major account. We were madly in love and having a great time."

But, it was in San Francisco where Simpson first felt the effects of financial strain.

"Ann gave up a fairly lucrative interior design job in St. Louis to be with me when we moved out West. So we went from two fairly good salaries in St. Louis to one salary in San Francisco. I was making about $37,000 at the time and our rent was $800 a month. Soon the financial pinch got to us. We lived in this beautiful area surrounded by all these great things but felt unable to take advantage of them. And Ann had always been a diehard St. Louis person. She had been a great sport, but after a year and a half, she was getting homesick."

After a brief stop in the Southeast, the Simpsons found their way back to the Gateway City with Simpson taking a job at a St. Louis ad agency, again working on agri-business. But then fate handed him an unexpected turn in his life.

"We got back to St. Louis in 1984. In 1987 Ann was diagnosed with cancer."

Despite the diagnosis, they bought their first home. Simpson enjoyed his work and being back in St. Louis, but he was getting burnt out—and pigeonholed—working solely on the agricultural business his entire career. He was ready for a change.

And, with a stroke of luck, he found the perfect job.

"I landed a job with a large consumer products company in their internal creative services group. It was a great opportunity for me because the group had overcapacity and was soliciting work from outside clients as well. They needed a salesman. My friend got me in the door and I schmoozed myself into a job."

Soon Simpson worked himself up to National Sales Manager for the group with five sales people scouring the U.S., promoting the unit's sales promotion, business meeting and video services.

"I absolutely *COULD NOT WAIT* to get to work in the morning. It was my favorite job ever," Simpson remembered fondly. "My boss and I absolutely clicked. It was the best time of my career and life. I still have my performance reviews from those years. On a scale of five, I consistently received four-point-nines."

Unfortunately, though, due to a family issue his boss eventually had to leave. Although he had recommended Simpson as his replacement, they brought in someone senior and older.

"It just wasn't the same anymore," Simpson explained, "so I talked to a friend and landed a job in consumer promotions. It wasn't like my previous job, but it was okay."

Despite Ann's cancer treatments, life was pretty good for the Simpsons at this time. "We were the classic DINKs. Double Income, No Kids. Ann went back to work in the interior design business when she could and we were living on one really good salary and one pretty good salary. We both drove new cars. We really didn't want kids. Our relationship, itself, sustained us."

In 1992, Ann finally succumbed to cancer.

"I was devastated, completely. When you lose someone like Ann, your career becomes very secondary," he reminisced. "One time she confided in me that she had told her therapist, 'I really hate it when Kurt works late.' Those words made me think and reevaluate. It was the biggest turning point in my life. It was time to reinvent myself. I told my therapist, 'I don't want to be a company man anymore.'"

Right after Ann passed, though, Simpson was told he was up for a prestigious product manager's job. So despite his intent to reinvent himself, he poured himself into his work to ensure that he would secure the position. However, ultimately the position was given to someone else by senior management dictate.

"It was kind of like a one-two punch, losing Ann and then the job. Losing Ann made me regret being a workaholic and losing the job reinforced that thought. I said to myself this is a message. Actually, it was a Godsend."

Simpson stayed at his old job and eventually got a promotion. During this time, he met his second wife, Jill. They married in 1995 and decided to start a family. A daughter was born in 1996 and a son in 1997.

In 1999 Jill and Kurt decided it was time to move out of St. Louis. "Jill and I were literally bumping into ghosts from my first marriage. We would run into one of my old friends on the street or at the mall, and he or she would look at Jill and say. 'Oh you must be Ann.' It was time to go, time for a fresh start. So I took a job as a promotion director at a fairly large financial services firm based again in the Midwest."

It was there where Simpson's finances—and subsequently marriage—took a sharp turn to the south.

"The company I worked for had a business model that didn't work in the digital age," Simpson explained. "I lasted there for four years, but inevitably was downsized out of a job."

After a fairly steady rise up the corporate ladder, for the first time in his career, Simpson found himself unemployed. "I was flabbergasted. Here I am, a smart guy, a competent guy with great experience and I'm out on the street. We wanted to stay in the Midwest, but the big companies there just weren't hiring. I looked for nine or ten months, living off savings and my 401K, and then finally got a call from a recruiter in Michigan."

The recruiter tried to twist his arm to take an interview with a healthcare company based in Michigan and owned by an incredibly wealthy entrepreneur with a track record of unparalleled success and a reputation for spending lavishly on employees. At first, Simpson resisted. "I told the recruiter I had never done healthcare and we weren't too crazy about moving to Michigan."

Soon thereafter, Simpson received a call from the company's owner. "I really want you for this job," he said, "be at the airport in the morning and I'll have my private jet pick you up."

The entrepreneur wined, dined and convinced Simpson he was the man for the job. The company was exploiting a growing niche within the healthcare field and they thought the sky was the limit.

"I was probably pulling down about $120,000 at my previous job and he gave me a $50,000 dollar raise. When we began looking for homes in the Michigan suburbs, though, reality set in. In the Midwest we lived in a great 3,000-square-foot home in a desirable neighborhood. We had paid $229,000 for it. The homes we saw in Michigan in that price range were terrible. No way would I ever let my kids live in a house like that. Comparable homes in Michigan ran about $500,000-plus. It was 2004, mortgage money was readily available, so we went for it."

Hindsight being 20/20, that proved to be the breaking point.

"My boss was an ex-senior executive from the auto industry. Together, we were running this healthcare business using direct-response TV as a lead generation vehicle. But we ran into a problem. Major hospitals in the area saw us succeeding and then offered the same services for about half the price. We tried to convince the owner to drop his price point, but he refused. He insisted that our services were better and we deserved the premium."

Despite Simpson's and his boss's repeated pleas that the owner drop his price or close down the business, each time they asked, he was would reply, "Fire three people."

"I saw the handwriting on the wall when I came to work one day and there were boxes outside my boss's office. The owner had let him go. Now I was a one-man show, literally running all the marketing programs myself. The owner even fired my ad agency without telling me. Finally, I told the owner to just shut it down.

"So here I was, for the second time in my life unemployed. I had a family to support and a gigunda mortgage to pay. My marriage was shaky. Our savings were almost nonexistent. Yet, we kept on living the same lifestyle as before."

Luckily, Simpson found a job at a consumer goods company in Minnesota within several months. He broke even on the house in Michigan and found a nice house for about the same price in Minnesota while pledging to economize on living expenses. However, Simpson was tired of all the moving, tired of the peaks and valleys of corporate America and tired of punching the clock for a paycheck.

"I was just too tired of dragging two kids around the country. The older I got, the more cynical I became. I got tired of working for a paycheck. It just wasn't me and my attitude showed through. I lasted about a year there and then I was canned. I remember one day shortly before that, my boss saw me in the hallway and said, 'You just don't look like you're happy working here.' You know what?" Simpson interjected. "He was right."

Again, Simpson was able to network himself into a job at another consumer products company, this time in Wisconsin. "It was really a good job for me, the types of things I have done for years and was really good at."

But, as Simpson would learn, being good at something doesn't necessarily guarantee success.

It's a Sunday afternoon in late Spring. Simpson has just spent two rigorous hours in the local park playing ball with his son. Proudly, he says, "For 55, I can still shag flies with the best of them. Some of those younger dads were huffin' and puffin' a lot more than I was."

Standing in his master bedroom, he looks out the window and surveys his affluent suburban Wisconsin neighborhood. "We bought this house last year at a foreclosure sale. We paid $475,000 and it appraised for $610,000. We bought the classic 'worst house in a good neighborhood.' There was a method to our madness, though. We thought that if we invested wisely in the house over time—putting in new furnaces, windows, siding, paint—we could get it up to the level of the rest of the neighborhood. The community is very desirable."

He points out the master bedroom window. "The house right across the street is worth $750,000; farther to the west, there's one worth $800,000. Within eyesight is a million-dollar home, and down the street is a two-million-dollar house. We always used to joke we were the Clampetts of the neighborhood."

But fate—and corporate America—threw a wrench in Simpson's plans. One and a half months after they closed on their new home, he was told his company would be moving his entire department to Illinois.

"We were shocked," he said. "We had crafted a plan to make a windfall on the house over time and now the plan was toast."

At the same time, Simpson's marriage was unraveling.

"It really began in Michigan. I got this big bump in salary and we began living like the cash would just keep on coming. We got used to a certain lifestyle and couldn't effectively cut back when the same amount of money wasn't there.

"Last March we crashed and burned. We were living beyond our means. We were going broke. I told Jill, 'I like my life, but I can't work any longer or harder. If we want to continue our lifestyle, you have to go back to work.' We had no savings to speak of. We were living paycheck to paycheck. It was the undoing of my marriage."

Simpson and his wife began the divorce process a year ago July and it became official in Spring 2009. Now he's still in the process of selling his house in Wisconsin and making two moves to Illinois (his wife agreed to move there as well in a separate residence so they could co-parent).

So was Simpson's downturn a result of the economic downturn?

"Yes and no," he answered. "We never took a home-equity loan against the house, but we did take on these monster mortgages. Money was easy and we kept borrowing and borrowing and borrowing as we went from house to house. I always had the mentality that I'll always keep on earning. I'm in the top echelon of income in the U.S. The housing market is always going to go up, I thought. In the end, it was just plain stupid to keep spending at that level."

Right now Simpson is braving the most stressful time of his life. He is a senior-level marketing executive at a large company with all the associated stresses and strains, he just completed the divorce process, financially he's sinking, he's preparing for two moves, and he's still living in his house with his ex-wife out of necessity.

"Stress?" he chuckled. "On a scale of 1 to 10, I'm at 27."

Despite a respectable income, he's juggling funds just to survive.

"I didn't pay the mortgage last month or the month before," he explained. "I'll get a default decree if I get 62 days behind. I'm struggling to make one more payment before the end of July, which would rescind the decree and cover me until September. At that point, my company will buy the house for about what I originally paid as part of my relocation package."

Despite all his moves, Simpson never made any real gains in the housing market. He depleted his 401K after his first layoff, and he has nothing in the bank.

"My kids just asked me if we could go out for a pizza tonight," he lamented, "and I had to say no."

The ups and downs of life in corporate America, easy credit, easy mortgage money, divorce, all of these factors contributed to Kurt Simpson's predicament, which begs the question: *How can someone with such obvious talent, a good career with several good jobs at good companies, end up this way? Do our giant companies pay enough in severance packages? Is it right to force people to deplete their 401Ks to support themselves and their families between jobs, particularly if they aren't covered by a traditional pension program?*

"I always joked that one day they're going to take me out of my office on a stretcher, but it's no longer a joke," Simpson told me. "I'll either be carted out or they'll fire me and I'll be living in a homeless shelter."

Despite a $150,000 salary and a potential $50,000 bonus, Simpson will have to stretch to get by when he and his ex-wife relocate to Illinois. "After all is said and done, after alimony and child support, I'll have $4,000 a month to live on and the rent on my apartment will suck up $1,500 of that. I gave my ex-wife my corporate moving expenses and I let her have the hi-def TV and SUV for the kids."

Then, of course, there's the inevitable question: What about the kids' higher education plans?

He took a deep breath, looked out his window, gazed upon the upper-middle-class neighborhood and responded somberly, "There's nothing in the bank for it. Nothing. That haunts me. My dad paid for all of my education and he was a plumber. It absolutely haunts me."

* * *

Chapter 7

Disrupting News

T*he generation of promise, Baby Boomers had a healthy head start— better educated, more socially aware and from more comfortable households than their parents' generation. Many are high achievers who've worked hard to attain their personal vision of this promise. But what happens when this vision becomes compromised by forces beyond one's control?*

* * *

"Disruptive?" Ian Stein raises an eyebrow as he sits at the AVID in his video editorial room. "Sure, I'd say it's disruptive. It's forcing me to reevaluate everything." Stein went on to explain, "I'm independent by nature. I've had my own business for 10 years. But this downturn has forced me to think about working for someone else again. And that's exactly what *I don't ever* want to do."

Stein, a thoughtful, introspective journalist, left a successful career in broadcast journalism to pursue his dream to become a documentary filmmaker. Of course, since the revenue generated by documentaries— no matter how insightful the content—pales in comparison to Hollywood blockbusters—no matter how vapid the content—Stein supplements his filmmaking with industrial video production and media training businesses.

"My video and media training businesses are both down severely," he said. "They're important to me because they pay the overhead that allows me to work on documentaries. I've had three projects cancel this year alone. Some of my industrial video contracts are with law-enforcement agencies and county governments. When they're told to tighten their belts, my stuff goes right out the window. It's the same way with corporate work, too."

Since childhood, Stein has been fascinated—perhaps *captivated* is more appropriate—by the space program. For the last six years, he's been working on a documentary about the Space Shuttle. For Stein, it's been a labor of love but quite laborious in a literal sense. "Beyond actually making the documentary, shooting interviews, finding stock footage and sitting at the video editing bay, I had to do a ton of work, pitching the idea to potential backers and aligning myself with people in the industry who would champion the film and could help get a back end-deal once the film is complete, lots of stuff."

It's not that Stein has anything *inherently* against working for a big company again, he had done it quite successfully for more than two decades, it's that it would compromise his life-long dream.

"I've worked six years on this film. It's been a painful process but also a learning process and, in many respects, a humbling process. It's almost done. I don't know what comes next. But if I had to go take another job, I would never be able to find out. That would be the real tragedy."

Originally, Ian thought he wanted to be a theater major, concentrating in lighting design. When he entered college, though, he became more interested in television and radio journalism, perhaps as a result of the times.

"The Vietnam war had a profound effect on me," said Stein. "I had a vested interest in politics because I was eligible for the draft. I was vehemently opposed to being drafted to fight a war I didn't believe in. This fueled my interest in journalism. It was a unique time, a time of social justice and civil rights. The other profound impact on my decision to go into journalism was my father's career as a print journalist. Every night, the conversation at the dinner table was politics and journalism. So I guess it was in my DNA by the time I got to college."

After graduation, Stein felt like he was ready to conquer the world, but today he is much more reflective about that time of his life. "When you first graduate, you think you're king of the world, you think you know everything, you've earned your right to jump in and lead the troops. But as Ted Koppel once said in a commencement address, 'you haven't earned anything yet.' I still don't consider myself fully mature and fully grown. You learn from the talented people around you. You learn that you don't know everything, that other people know more. It's very humbling, but I have to say when I finally came to that realization, it was the most significant event in my career."

And learn he did. Stein began his career as a desk assistant, basically a glorified gofer, at a major TV station in Washington, D.C. He loved the excitement of working the desk, seeing news happen as it developed and helping to shape the way it was reported. But he realized he wasn't quite ready for prime time yet. He was advised by an executive producer to go to a smaller market where he could learn from his mistakes. So Stein landed in Orlando.

In Orlando Stein became a full-fledged producer and each night was responsible for putting together the 11 and eventually the 6 o'clock newscasts. Two years later, he graduated to Miami where he produced the 11 o' clock news and then was asked to completely rebuild their

5:30 newscast. But his ultimate goal was to get back to D.C., where the real action was.

"I got a job at the Metromedia station in D.C. in 1982," he told me. "My job was to produce the 10 o'clock news, which was a real disaster. They had horrible ratings, they hadn't invested much. But now they wanted me to come in and spice it up. I was the kid from Miami, a hot market known for fast-paced news. It was a great time in my career. We completely changed the tempo of the broadcast, brought in a new high-profile anchor, and within a few months doubled the ratings. Soon we were the number-one-rated prime-time news show in the country. I was promoted to managing editor and I won my first Emmy."

But then, of course, just when things seemed to be going along smoothly, everything became disrupted by a change in management. "Fox bought the station in 1986 and, yeah, we had all those meetings where they assured us that 'only the name on the check will change.' But within several weeks, everyone in top management was gone."

Interestingly, the person they brought in to be news director had known Stein in his previous life as a desk assistant during his first job in D.C. Stein thought it was important to be proactive with his new boss. "I took her out to lunch and said, 'You only know me as a gofer, not as a producer.' I went on to tell her. 'I'm not the same Ian Stein you knew six years ago. If you look at me that way, just fire me now. Otherwise give me a chance.' It was risky, but she became one of the most significant mentors in my career."

Stein hung on at Fox for another year, but his dream was always to get back to his original station in D.C. "They hired me back to produce the weekend newscasts, which weren't doing very well. Soon, I earned a reputation as 'the news doctor.' I was a disruptive force. I would take the newscasts that weren't doing well, analyze them, then blow them up and rebuild them."

After that, Stein went on to special projects producing, mostly working on special feature series to be run on the newscasts during 'sweep periods,' when the rating companies measure the viewership of the newscast. "I became the 'utility infielder' for the news department. If there was ever a problem, they would say, 'Grab Stein. He'll make it happen.'"

Although a driven man, Stein's life was not all work and no play. At a party in 1985, he met his future wife, Micki. "She was in broadcasting at an all-news radio station in D.C., so I knew her by reputation. We dated for a couple of years, even though she had decided to do a fellowship program at Columbia University in business journalism. We got married in 1987, and she took a job in government on Capitol Hill as a communications director, then later in the Clinton Administration. Now she works as an Executive Vice President at public relations firm that specializes in government relations. I'd say she's pretty successful."

Stein was also successful throughout the 1990s—he won four more Emmys for his feature segments on medical issues—but he began to get antsy. "It came to a climax when there was an executive producer opening at the station. I applied for it and pitched hard to station management. They kept on telling me, 'If we promote you, we're going to have to find a new utility guy.' I was the victim of my own success."

One evening, Stein remembers whining to his wife that he would be stuck at the same station doing the same job for the rest of his life.

The next day, he did something impulsive.

"I went into work and quit. Just like that," he recalled proudly. "I had money saved up, the economy was great. My wife was supportive. She had a great job. We had no kids. I had always wanted to produce a documentary on the space program. So what the heck?"

Stein pitched his idea to a production company and worked with them on developing it for seven months. During this time, he moonlighted as a freelance producer, developing video news releases for public relations firms. When the deal with the production company did not work out, he invested some of his own funds to finance his project. Now after six years of hard work, the documentary is almost done.

But Stein finds himself at a crossroads.

"I need to make a decision about what's next," Stein said. "I know what I *want* to do—I want to make another documentary—but because of the economy I might have to do something different. And, to me, that would be a tragedy."

A classic DINK couple, you would think that Ian and Micki Stein would be relatively unaffected by the downturn, but that's not the case. "Our investments are in the toilet. At one point a financial advisor told us we were in good shape to retire by 65, but now I don't want to even think about it. I can't even begin to predict when we'll be able to retire, if ever."

Luckily, they invested in a beach property in 2000, just before the real estate market took off. "That property is our anchor. Even though it's down a bit, it's our anchor along with our home. Everything else will take years to come back."

How else has the downturn affected your life?

"Well, we never really had an extravagant lifestyle," Stein answered. "My wife earns a good income, but my share of the household income is down dramatically, so I spend a lot less."

Predictably, with the downturn came a fair amount of stress.

"The stress is huge," Stein said. "I've lost a ton of work. There's an incredible amount of pressure on me to meet my financial goals for my business. Last year I didn't meet them. This year I'm not going to meet them either. And working on the film has taken me away from my clients."

The Steins live in a relatively modest four-bedroom colonial in a middle class neighborhood in the suburbs. "What I like about our neighborhood is its diversity. It's enriched with people from all different types of backgrounds, ethnically, lifestyle-wise, everything. It sort of mirrors my career because I strongly believe we learn from the people around us."

As we sat in his in-home video editing room, I asked a probing question.

Okay, so here you are, in some ways a typical Baby Boomer, one with dreams and aspirations. You put in your time—more than two decades at a successful broadcast journalism career. You thought your retirement was safe. You quit a stable job to pursue your dream. How do you feel about the forces that may have robbed you of both your dream and your future?

He didn't hesitate. "We live in a selfish technology-driven, shortcut-driven culture and the chicken's come home to roost. A lot of it is cultural. We grew up in a culture of greed, a culture of, 'I gotta have it now, I gotta have everything I want and I'm not gonna stop until I get it.' That's what happened to the banking industry and the mortgage industry. Everyone wanted a shortcut. They come up with these fabulous too-good-to-be-true mortgage deals and no one thought about the long-term consequences. Now the chicken's come home to roost and everything's falling through the roof."

Animatedly, Stein pulls an object from his pocket, his iPhone. "When I coach executives in media training, the first thing I do is put this on the table and tell him or her, 'The world has changed. This is the symbolic turning point. It puts extraordinary power in the palm of your hand, the ability to upload or download information wherever and whenever you want.' If you stretch that thought to who we are as a culture—the I-want-everything-now mentality—it explains a lot. Technology has helped feed the beast."

But wait a minute, you mean to tell me you're not absolutely furious at those in the banking industry who may have shattered your dream and jeopardized your future?

"But we're all responsible for it," he answered. "Our own personal behavior has driven this. Yeah, you can point your finger at the banking industry, the Reagan years of deregulation, but ultimately we're all responsible. It all goes back to this cultural issue of greed. If we didn't have this drive to always have it now, we wouldn't be in this mess."

What do you think about a recovery?

"I think people's expectations about the recovery are completely wrong," he answered. "I think people are expecting the economy to recover within months. Personally, I think it will be years. It has to do with the cultural undercurrent of 'gotta have it now, there's no waiting in line.' I think people will eventually lose faith in government and the people who are trying to fix things—they might not have enough time to right the ship."

How do you think Obama is handling things?

"I think he's on the right path. But I fear that because of the way we do business in politics and media today, he might not get the chance to head down that path."

As a broadcast journalism professional, Stein is in a unique position to give his thoughts on how media and politics intermix. "Everything's driven by the 24-hour news cycle. The people making the decisions are not seasoned people. A lot of them are young. I think about when I first started—no one would ever give me a job like that so quickly. They're not focusing on editorial, they're more focused on showmanship and ratings. The current healthcare debate is a good example. A lot of the opposition is based on out-and-out incorrect facts designed to stimulate anger and get ratings."

So what's the future hold for Ian Stein?

"I want to finish my documentary. I want to see what's around the corner. I don't want to be forced to do anything I don't want to do because of the economy. I want to make another film. Even though retirement may be far off, I don't really want to retire. I want to work, but I want to do the work that I want to do."

An idealistic, introspective Boomer who has scrambled around from TV station to TV station and from market to market to cut his teeth in broadcast journalism, Stein has in many respects earned the right to pursue his dream. But forces far beyond his control may prevent that from happening.

Is that a true tragedy or just how life unfolds? Do Boomers feel an entitlement to pursue their dreams, an entitlement that previous generations never even imagined? It's hard to tell.

But who knows?

Maybe Ian Stein's loss can turn into society's gain.

Maybe those 24-hour news cycles can benefit from a disruptive force once again presiding over things in the newsroom.

* * *

Chapter 8

New Beginnings

*I*f hard work equated proportionally to success, John Perrotti would be a multimillionaire today. Whenever he's set his sights on something, he's done everything in his power to go for it. He's been an aspiring filmmaker, a caterer, an actor, a Wall Street trader, a partner in a successful trading firm and a bartender. He's been successful at times and at other times, not, but he's never let hard luck or hard times get in the way of hard work.

* * *

The area is nestled comfortably, if not abruptly, smack in the gut of Fairfield County, Connecticut. It's like an urban wart festering within the pristine suburbs of the super-affluent: McMansions, investment bankers, hedge fund managers, CEOs and the like abound within a stone's throw. As one walks cautiously through the neighborhood past the police station, the bail bondsman's storefront, the Hispanic tavern, the disheveled apartment buildings, a few homeless people clutching onto their shopping cart homes, you're quickly transported from urban blight to gentrified heaven, a major discontinuity, like stepping onto the 3 train in Brownsville and getting off in the West Village—or maybe stepping onto the back lot of a Hollywood studio with all its disparate surprises.

Stumbling onto something unexpected, you walk past turn-of-the-century retail and industrial structures, meticulously restored, housing all sorts of restaurants, boutiques, coffee shops and galleries. It's an upscale street of cobblestone walkways, faux gaslights and colorful facades.

On Wednesdays through Saturdays, you can find a standard neighborhood fixture tending bar right behind the window in the fashionable Northern Italian restaurant near the end of the street, John Perrotti. He's an earthy, young-looking 48, with jet black hair slicked back and stubble growing on his cheeks and neck. Wearing either a knit retro-bowling or plaid cotton shirt, along with his standard jeans and sneakers, he's there working dutifully, sort of an in-between type character. He can be gruff and even caustic at times, but inside, John's a teddy bear, your best friend once you open up to each other.

"My best year on Wall Street, I made high six figures," he explained as he shook a jigger for an Appletini. "Those were great days back then. Eventually a few partners and I started our own firm, and we had this trading business with offices on Broad Street and Broadway."

The restaurant has a homey, rustic décor—exposed brick walls, industrial metal duct work snaking its way around the wooden beams hanging overhead, a shiny, highly lacquered bar forged from a natural piece of burly red oak. The regulars are as diverse as the décor—a bunch of gasoline traders and advertising guys from the gentrified office building next door, the female architect from across the street, the African American Wall Street IT guy from the apartment upstairs, the hulking British wine cellar designer/builder, the octogenarian coffee merchant from upstate and, of course, a steady stream of yuppie couples from the surrounding suburbs looking for haute cuisine at not-so-haute prices.

"Yeah, we had a real thing going for a while," Perrotti mused as he contemplatively leaned on the bar, "but sooner or later the partnership got too difficult to manage, so we split up."

Perrotti's story began in the suburban, post-war town of East Islip, Long Island. It wasn't quite a Levittown, Perrotti explained, because the "houses were bigger in East Islip—split levels—and the lots were bigger—a third of an acre," but it definitely was within the same phylum of community. "It was the type of town people came to for new starts, new beginnings."

In East Islip, Perrotti endured what was perhaps the most significant experience of his life. "I was only 11 when my father passed away," he told us. "It left me in a house with three women, my mom and two of my three sisters."

"My dad was in the Navy for 21 years. In 1971 he was diagnosed with cancer. Although there wasn't a cure, they tried cobalt radiation treatment. First at St. Albans in Queens. Then he went down to another hospital in Florida and passed away. He died only eight months after his initial diagnosis."

Understandably, this life-altering event left a critical imprint on Perrotti. "Most of my learning experiences during those years were through my friends, there were a lot of kids my age growing up in the neighborhood, mostly Catholic and Jewish.

"It was tough watching my mother work so hard to support us. She worked every day at a coat factory. Even though my dad was retired Navy, the pensions weren't insured. You had to pay every month to insure it, like life insurance. They couldn't afford the payments, so when he died, his pension went with him. There were no survivorship benefits. Add to that both my mother and father were notch babies [a term used to refer to U.S. citizens born between 1917 and 1921 whose Social Security benefits are calculated by a different lower-yielding formula than for those born before 1917], so her Social Security benefits weren't as good as they could have been."

At the behest of his high school guidance counselor, Perrotti began thinking about what he wanted to do with his life. "I was sort of unfocused back then," he recalled. "You know, they force you to choose something, but you don't really know. I ended up going to SUNY Alfred, a two-year school. At first I was a little lost, but in my second year I had this history professor whom I just loved. He became my mentor and helped focus me. I decided I wanted to go to film school. He helped me look for colleges. He was pushing me toward Cornell, but it didn't have a great film program. So I decided to go to San Francisco State."

Although he commuted into the city from Marin County, Perrotti loved everything about the San Francisco area, with one exception. "The school was going through budget restrictions and I never really clicked with the instructors," he explained. "I went from an environment at Alfred where I had a supportive mentor to an art school where instructors wanted you to do it their way."

Not long thereafter, John's career went through a quick segue from the cinematic arts to the culinary arts. "My friend's parents were having a wine and cheese party at their home and they asked me to help out. I guess they thought I did a pretty good job because they started recommending me around and it grew into a business."

Although John went on to earn his degree at San Francisco State, he had become disillusioned with the film program. However, he was anything but disillusioned about earning income through catering. "Things started to take off after I graduated. Here I was a kid in my early 20s, earning decent income and owning a small company with actual employees. I never thought I'd have anything like that."

But soon Perrotti's career path fast forwarded in another direction. "I was getting a little bored in San Francisco and I started getting the acting bug. So I took some acting courses and decided to pick up and move back to New York. I always thought it would be cool to live in Manhattan. I started living with my sister on the Upper West Side, then moved down to the East Village."

At that point in time—the mid-1980s—the East Village was not what one would call a gentrified area. "It was a jungle, every man for himself down there. I would step over all sorts of people and things when I went back to my apartment at night. In San Francisco everything was so neat and clean. The East Village was so much the opposite, but an exciting opposite. My friend and I got a place on East 9th Street, between 1st and 2nd Avenues, a basement apartment in an old carriage house. You had everything in that building—artists, transvestites, gays, straights, even a little preppy element starting to slip in; it was sort of the *Bright Lights, Big City* era."

Like many of his neighbors, Perrotti pursued his acting passion. "I got some pretty good referrals to acting teachers. But I found they were all teaching the same old thing—a scene from *Our Town*, a scene from *Picnic*, the same old crap."

Still, Perrotti went through the process of getting head shots taken, going to auditions and paying all the necessary dues that a fledgling actor in New York City had to pay. At the same time, he pursued video. "I took classes at Global Village in SoHo. They had a three-camera studio set up. Some friends of mine in a band wanted to shoot a video, so I got my chance—I shot an actual music video." Then he paused and smiled. "And you know what? The video aired on TV. The band used it on *The Joe Franklin Show* on Channel 9 to promote themselves."

But there's a constant stumbling block for artists, and its color is green.

He chuckled: "I never realized that all my artistic desires would teach me so much about the restaurant business."

To make ends meet, Perrotti found himself doing the same things that most aspiring actors in New York City do—bartending, waiting tables and juggling schedules to fit in auditions. "Working in restaurants is about the only thing you can do to be able to fit in all the other stuff," he explained.

Perrotti savored those years, though. "I was basically doing everything I ever wanted to do, pursuing my interests and passions. One of my instructors asked me to help her with lighting on a video project. We filmed at the NYU pool and the piece appeared at MOMA for a while. I thought I was making headway in the business at that point. But then you run into a stumbling block; you have no money and instead of putting time in at the studio or acting class, you're picking up an extra shift at the bar because the rent's coming due."

During this period, he met his wife, an NYU film school grad. Like him, she was looking for work and bartending in SoHo on the side. They married in 1993 and moved to Brooklyn. "Life was good back then," Perrotti reminisced.

Another significant event in Perrotti's life happened at that time as well. "A friend of mine worked as a clerk on the floor of the Stock Exchange. He invited me down one day to watch, and I absolutely fell in love with it. Soon I found myself reading less about film and acting and more about business and finance. I decided to go back to school to get a degree in finance. I registered at Pace. Most of the art courses that I had previously taken did not apply, so I basically had to redo the whole four years."

"Those were busy times," he recalled. "I don't know how my wife and I ever saw each other. I went to school night and day and during the summer. I'd study on the train, then at home until 3 a.m. and be up for a 7 a.m. class, all this while working two jobs bartending about

50 hours a week. But somewhere in between, my wife got pregnant and we had a baby, my son, Sam."

After all that hard work, Perrotti did not find the post-graduation job market in finance so welcoming. "Basically, the Wall Street firms wanted young kids in their 20s. Here I was this ex-actor-filmmaker-bartender in his mid-30s, fresh out of college, and I just didn't fit their mold.

"One day a cousin of mine who ran a trading desk for a big Wall Street firm had me come over to watch. I watched him work his desk, his computer, his phone, and I was absolutely hooked. He told me to ask questions if I couldn't follow something, but I understood everything. I finally knew what I wanted to do with my life.

"I found this firm on Wall Street that would teach people to trade, but you had to put up your own capital. I really wanted to do it. Everyone told me I was stupid and ignorant, and I was in effect paying for a job that probably wouldn't work out. The more people who told me I was heading in the wrong direction, the more I wanted to do it. So I begged, borrowed and stole and came up with the 20 grand I needed to get started."

Needless to say, Perrotti's obsession with trading consumed him. "This was a full-time commitment. I had to quit my other two jobs. I'd be at my desk at seven in the morning and not leave until seven at night. At first, it was very, very tough."

"There are three steps to making money in trading," he explained. "First you're net negative and gross negative. That means you're negative to the market and negative on your broker commission. The next step you become net positive, but still you're gross negative—you're beginning to win against the market, but you're still in the red on commissions. Finally, you become both net and gross positive. That's when you start making money.

"I sat at my desk for seven months watching my capital account dwindle as I learned the ropes. Finally in March 1998 I became both net and gross positive. It couldn't come soon enough because I was down to $1,200 in my capital account."

So how did he survive during the interim?

"I had absolutely no income for those seven months, but fortunately my credit was good. I had a bunch of credit cards. I would take a cash advance at the beginning of each month and pay all my bills. Then I'd pay the monthly minimum on each card. It was a shell game. We basically lived on nothing."

Perrotti explained that making money at trading is both an art and science. "You have to learn all the tricks that the market makers play against you and how they try to deceive you. It's a game out there and they're all playing it. You have to learn how to play. It doesn't necessarily require a bull market. A trader likes volatility in either direction. You can make money long or short. My cousin used to tell me, 'Short first and ask questions later.'"

After he got over the initial hurdles, Perrotti proved to be a natural at his craft. "Like I said, I made a lot of money trading. My best year was 2000, I earned high six figures. But it's very, very draining. It's a battle every day. You could see how hard it is on people by just watching the guys around you."

"A lot of things were going on in my life back then. My wife and I were planning on buying a house. We hadn't focused exactly on where, but we finally settled on Connecticut."

Moving his family to another state wasn't the only change in Perrotti's life.

"The company my colleagues and I were working for had made a lot of promises: 'We'll let you run a desk. You can teach people how to trade. We'll give you a percentage of the commissions they make.' After a while, it became obvious we were helping them grow but they were doing nothing for us, they were reneging on everything. So a bunch of us got together and decided to start a small firm. The idea was for us to bring new traders in, teach them the rules of the road, then eventually withdraw from trading ourselves and live off the commissions. That's how you make real money in this business."

In a business where timing is everything, though, time may not have been completely on their side. "We signed our lease on Broad Street in July 2001 and watched the planes hit the World Trade Center a few months later. You know, we had a second office a few blocks away on Broadway on the 31st floor. One of the guys went out on the balcony for a cigarette right before the plane crashed. The plane came so close to him that he could look into the cockpit and actually see the face of the terrorist who was flying the plane. When it hit the Trade Center, the heat singed his hair. I'll never forget that.

"They put us all in a temporary shelter that morning. Then later in the afternoon they let us go. A handful of us walked to where the Trade Center was, this was before they came up with the term Ground Zero. It was terrible, disgusting. We were all covered in soot, talking to the firemen and watching stuff burn."

On the business front, things weren't perfect, but he and his partners were surviving. "After 9/11, yeah, business got tough, but not as tough as you might think. A lot of people made a lot of money after 9/11 because the markets became turbulent. Traders like market turbulence. I was one of four managing partners. A lot of seasoned traders came with us from the previous company and they were all minority partners."

Over the next two years John and his partners successfully grew their business. "At the height of it, we had 150 traders, 16 full-time employees and 36 partners. We had two offices in New York, another in Miami and small one in Westhampton."

He went on to tell me that his company traded approximately 100 million shares a month and had about $9 million in regulatory capital, yielding the firm about $55 million in intra-day buying power.

Impressive. So did you live the 'high life,' partaking of that continuous stream of sex drugs and rock 'n roll that the conventional wisdom associates with Wall Street success?

"I heard lots of crazy stories back then," he answered, "drugs, women, partying, all that stuff, but I wasn't really part of it. Yeah, I made decent money, but I had a family to support. I was able to pay off a lot of the debt I had accumulated over the previous years. And just as the business was peaking, my family had to move because a fire upstairs in our building in Brooklyn caused smoke damage to our apartment. We rented a pretty big house in Connecticut and that wasn't cheap. Sure, at times, it was nice to fly back and forth to Miami and stay in a suite at the Loews, but that's about as much of the 'high life' as I experienced."

As one of the managing partners, John was responsible for the overall operations of the business and partnership; one turned out to be a much more difficult task than the other. "Running the partnership was troublesome," he told me. "A handful of traders, who were limited partners, thought they should be on the board of directors. They wanted us to give them a lower commission rate, a rate comparable to what they would get at a much larger firm that had much more buying power. I mean, we were only talking fractions of pennies...."

He paused for a moment, then continued. "Sometimes people are just ugly human beings. When they're unhappy they want to make everyone else unhappy. The few of them tried to recruit some others. They either wanted lower rates or out of their contracts. But if we let them go, our regulatory capital and buying power would go down, resulting in higher commission rates for those remaining and a more narrow profit spread. Eventually, the partnership became unmanageable."

With the partnership coming undone, Perrotti and his fellow board members had to make a difficult decision. "I never wanted to end it, but there were other partners who controlled more shares than I did and they didn't want to do it anymore. We took a vote, and the vote was to get out of everything and end the partnership. We took a really big hit. We had big deposits on space that we lost. All the computers were on lease. We had to return them and take stiff penalty hits. If we could have done another six months, we would have been out of all the leases. Everything came at a bad time."

So you had a successful business with all these traders, offices and buying power, and because of a few disgruntled partners, you shut it down. You say that somewhat smugly. Didn't it hurt?

Perrotti holds a lot inside, it's very evident. "Yeah, it hurt. Part of me really loved what I was doing and it was tough to get out of it. But in another way, it was a relief. I was glad I didn't have to manage the whole partnership anymore. It was a long time in the making. It's tough to be around unhappy, miserable people all the time."

At the same time, other things in Perrotti's life were coming undone.

"As the business unraveled, so did my marriage, and then my mom passed away. Up until we closed the business, I was making pretty good money. But the stress became unbearable; between the business, my mother and my marriage, it was a real pressure cooker."

At that point, the bubble burst.

"My wife and I separated, and I got my own place. I started trading from home, but hated it. You need to be around other traders to feel the buzz and pulse of the market. So, here I was. I wasn't making any money at home and I had two households to maintain instead of one. Money was flowing out, but not coming in. I probably should have declared bankruptcy in 2004 or 2005. It was much easier back then, before Bush changed the law. I tried to find a job at a big firm on Wall

Street, but being a trader for so long, I didn't have the skill sets they were looking for. They would ask me questions like, 'How good are you at Excel? How good are your graphing skills?' Geez, I had people doing these things for me in our business. Eventually, I came to the conclusion that I was highly skilled and highly un-hirable."

"So what could I do?" he asked rhetorically, standing behind the burly red oak bar and in front of a wall rack filled with exotic wines, liquors and beers. "I took a job catering and a few months later got my job here. I figured I'd do this until I could find something better."

The house is staid and gray on a middle-class street in a middle-class town in Fairfield County right off a county highway that leads to a state highway that leads to Interstate 95. There's a Korean nail place and Chinese dry cleaner down the road, then a strip mall with a deli, Chinese and Italian restaurants and an ATM across the way; the local cops hang out in the triangular parking lot when they have nothing better do. On the other side of the highway, behind the state of Connecticut's longest, most nerve-wracking red light, there's a Greek pizzeria that's very greasy, but very good, most patrons admit.

The house's porch flakes gray paint as do the six rickety wooden steps leading up to it. On the right side of the house juts an almost unexpected appendage, definitely not organic. It's wrapped around by an unfinished wooden staircase, connecting two metal storm doors, each with a small living quarters behind.

The second-floor apartment is Perrotti's.

"Yeah, this is home," he told me

But how did it all happen so quickly—from high six-figure Wall Street trader to struggling bartender?

"I hadn't made any real money since 2003. We lived paycheck to paycheck, supplemented by savings. I supported two houses, medical insurance, life insurance, everything. By the time you realize you're stuck at this income level, you're under water from trying to maintain the lifestyle of your old income level."

So did the downturn of 2008/2009 play a role in his current circumstances?

"Yes and no," he answered. "I've had my money out of the market for a long time. The restaurant I bartend at is doing pretty well because they offer good food at a moderate price. So, in those ways, it hasn't affected me. Where it's affected me is that my ex is making a lot less money, so I contribute more there. She lost her health coverage, so I've been trying to help with that. But it looks like we'll lose it completely. Even though the Obama Administration is picking up 65% of COBRA it will still be $630 per month and we just can't afford it. And, then, of course, today's economy makes it hard for me to get out of this mess. I want to open up another trading company, but there's no investor money out there. Everybody's scared and hoarding their cash."

Perrotti is an early riser, up at 6. The days he has Sam, he drives him to school to arrive at 7:05. Then he comes home, reads and searches the Internet for ideas, projects, anything that might make him money. Then he might do a few chores around his house, maybe go over to his ex-wife's to help fix her car or something, things he might have paid someone else to do during his salad days.

At 4 o'clock, he's behind the bar again.

"Yep, that's the way it is right now," he says as he pours another glass of Pinot Grigio.

There's something about John Perrotti. You would think from his background that he would be fast and slick, a mover and a shaker, a player; but that's not him at all. He holds a lot inside. Even when he's caustic, he's laid back. When asked about a celebrity he once knew, he didn't flinch a bit, just wiped the bar down and calmly uttered: *"Scumbag."*

No emotion, just the facts.

He's been through several new beginnings. He essentially attended college twice. He's worked his tail off to pursue his dreams, sometimes succeeding and sometimes failing, yet he was always willing to work hard to achieve his goals.

He's a proud father, loves his son. Together they do a lot. He shuttles Sam around to baseball, football and hockey practices and takes him into the city occasionally to see their beloved Mets. On a hot August day they might drive to Long Island, watch the Jets practice at Hofstra University, then travel on to Jones Beach.

"He's a good kid, real good" Perrotti boasted in that understated way of his. "But I had to support myself through college on student loans and that's what he's going to have to do."

But how about Sam's beloved dad and his retirement?

Perrotti paused for a moment and leaned on the bar. "I try not to think about it too much," he answered. "Here's what I know and how I see it." He became more animated. "I'm not going to retire by going to work for someone at a company. I'm too old. Putting away money at that pace, it just isn't going to accumulate."

So again, I ask, how?

He half smiles, his eyes glimmer. "The only way I'm going to retire is to get into a project and work it to death."

In this observer's estimation, he probably will.

* * *

Chapter 9

Jeep Thrills

S ometimes you do everything right and things still come out wrong—or, *in this case, almost wrong. John and Georgia Albee form a self-made New Jersey couple who are partners in two auto dealerships. Through hard work, they earned a good living for themselves, but as the economy crumbled, the toll it took on the U.S. auto industry almost brought them down.*

* * *

"It was absolutely, positively the scariest time of our lives," John Albee admitted as he skipped a stone across the wide river bordering the grounds to their New Jersey home. "We could have literally lost everything."

Albee is a self-made man. An aspiring Major League Baseball player in high school and college who tried out with the Cincinnati Reds, he leveraged his B.S. in accounting into various jobs in the auto industry until he worked himself up to partner of a local dealership group. He and his wife, Georgia—a self-made couple—were married right after he graduated Fairleigh Dickinson University and have been partners ever since—in business as well as life. To them, the meltdown could have destroyed the way of life they worked so hard to achieve. One of the dealerships that John's group owned was Chrysler Jeep.

In early 2009 Chrysler was teetering on bankruptcy.

"It's painful to even think about," Albee reminisced, "to think that if Chrysler went bankrupt or decided to terminate our dealership, everything we worked so hard for in life could've gone kaput, just like that."

"It wasn't great for our relationship either," Georgia interjected. "Every night John would come home stressed out and exhausted. He was distant, didn't want to talk. I was afraid to say boo because everything I said irritated him. He was always in a bad mood. I hate watching the news, but I was watching it every day. I was so wrapped up in the whole bankruptcy thing wondering if we would lose our business, I couldn't even eat."

The story of John and Georgia Albee is one of partnership, pursuit, crisis, success and, of course, love. Inseparable since right after they first met (well, actually, after the second time they met; they dated for a bit, then lost touch for several months only to be reunited one fateful night in a rickety old bar called The Locker Room in northern New Jersey). Although in their mid-50s, John and Georgia share the youthful exuberance and joie de vivre of a couple in their 20s. Tall and lanky, John still has the lithe frame of the short stop/second basemen he once was. When his once-dark curly hair started thinning, he decided to go all the way to bald, and he's been that way ever since. Petite and full of energy and spunk, Georgia has a cute cherubic face with a hint of youthful freckles. Each plays a masterful ying to the other's yang.

Both children of the 1960s, John and Georgia reacted in markedly different ways to the social mores of the times. "When I was in high school, my sister and I were crazy," Georgia recalled. "We did all sorts of drugs. When I was 14, my older brother wanted me to run away with him and go to Woodstock. I didn't, but it was sure tempting. Before I met John, I wanted to be a surgeon. I went to college for one year, not even knowing at the time that John was at the same school, but I did nothing but smoke pot. I stopped smoking and doing drugs right after that. As for John, he was focused on baseball at the time. He was on a different wavelength than everybody else."

When it became evident that John would not become the next Joe Morgan or Rogers Hornsby, he fell back on his accounting degree and got a job as an internal auditor at Uniroyal. As he traveled around the country auditing the company's operations, Albee grew bored. But something significant happened on one of his many plane trips. "I was sitting next to this guy and we talked almost the entire flight. Right before we landed, he said to me, 'You seem like you're the aggressive type. You want to be successful. You should read this book.' It was *Think and Grow Rich* by Napoleon Hill. Reading that book was a life-altering experience for me. I came to the conclusion that I needed to be in my own business. I needed to change course toward a path that would lead me into opening my own business."

John's first choice was real estate. Both Georgia and he pursued their licenses and then worked for a firm in Northern New Jersey. "Interest rates were really high back then," Georgia said, "like 16% and 18%. We were doing well but not well enough. Then I got pregnant, so it was time for John to get a real job."

Albee thought the auto business would be a good fit. "So I went around to the local auto dealerships and asked where their regional offices were located," Albee recalled. "The guy at the local Toyota dealership was really helpful. He told me, 'I know everyone over there, let me make a call.' He made a call right on the spot and I went through several interviews and eventually received an offer to be a management trainee."

Albee's first job was as a field service representative. From there, he was promoted to sales representative. "I forged some good relationships with dealers when I was in the field," he told me. "I saw these guys making a lot of money, and although I liked and respected them, I didn't think they were any smarter than me. They just had the money to open a store. Our problem was that we had no money."

So how did he eventually get his own dealership?

"It didn't happen directly," Georgia told me. "We met John's future partner on a Toyota dealer trip to Japan. They talked about eventually working together at some point in the future."

After eight years, John was no longer happy at Toyota. "I just didn't see it happening there," he said. So on the recommendation of one of his dealer-friends, he accepted a job with upstart Korean automaker Hyundai. "They were just entering the market. It seemed like there was lots of opportunity."

John and Georgia packed up the family, now including two sons, and moved about 80 miles away in New Jersey to be near Hyundai's regional headquarters.

There is where opportunity eventually knocked.

"The fellow that we met on the trip to Japan—John's eventual partner—had a plot of land in the area and was looking to put in a Hyundai dealership," Georgia explained. "They talked for two or three years about John eventually running the dealership and having an ownership interest. Finally, they came to an agreement and we achieved our lifelong dream."

As the dealership grew, they added Mitsubishi and Chrysler Jeep franchises as well. "But it was a difficult time for the business in general," John explained. "We were so new to it and we didn't know what we know today."

Ironically, it was Chrysler Jeep, the franchise they were in fear of losing in 2009, that propelled the Albees' early success.

"In 1993, when Jeep introduced the Grand Cherokee, things turned around for us," Georgia said. "It was the perfect car for the time, the first sport utility vehicle geared for everyday lives—soccer moms, dads, everybody. Going forward, we became more and more successful."

Life for the Albees, though, was not without its bumps in the road.

"In 1996 our oldest son's best friend got involved in drugs and committed suicide," Georgia recalled sadly. "We were devastated. He was like another son to us, went on vacations with us, spent a lot of his time at our house. It's 13 years later and we're still not completely over it."

Then 9/11 struck, an epochal event for all Baby Boomers.

"We were scared shitless," John said. "The next Saturday, a good friend of ours died of cancer. Those two events made us re-examine things. We were making good money, we weren't spending a lot. We had been visiting Georgia's sister up in Vermont for more than 20 years. We thought it would be a good idea to buy a place there. It would be our refuge away from a major metropolitan area if we ever got nuked."

And what a refuge they found—a spacious contemporary redwood home with a large comfortable deck shaded by a dense cluster of sugar maples. Covering a full 160 acres in northern Vermont, the Albees' property includes a 300-square-foot garage and an old-fashioned New England barn.

"During the worst days, when we didn't know if we would lose everything else, I told Georgia, 'We could always move to Vermont,'" John said somberly. "Not a bad worse-case scenario, I guess."

The Albees sensed that things weren't quite right well before the meltdown of 2008/2009. "Our business peaked in 2004/2005 and then it gradually slowed. We started to lose income, but we weren't really worried. We were still making good money, just not as much as before. Back in 2007, Chrysler started to have problems. They stopped leasing altogether and were very restrictive on who they would loan money to. Then in 2008, the real estate market got ugly and people began defaulting on their credit obligations," John Albee told me.

Of course, with the real estate market and the general economy in decline, the domestic automobile industry, which was already weak, got that much weaker.

When Albee first sensed Chrysler might be in real trouble, he changed his dealership's business model. "Of course, when you first hear things you tend to minimize them," he said. "We heard initial rumblings that Chrysler might declare bankruptcy in Fall 2008. In response to those rumors, we changed our business model from selling new cars to used cars. It worked out really well. Our service department's business was strong and our other businesses were doing pretty well."

At that time Albee decided to make another big change in his business model.

"The Mitsubishi dealership was just not pulling its weight," he told me. "Their national sales were getting worse and worse and worse. They weren't willing to provide advertising support and the other manufacturers were just eating them up. My partners and I decided it was cheaper to shut it down than keep it going."

Then they got the news they were hoping would never come— Chrysler had officially decided to declare bankruptcy.

"Those were three months of pure hell," Albee said. "There was so much talk, so much conversation. We constantly had conference calls with Chrysler's top execs. They kept on reassuring us, 'Take more product, we need to move more iron so we could come out of this.' At one point we had 500 or 600 cars on our lot. That was soaking up $80,000 a month in interest alone.

"There were two types of uncertainty we were dealing with back then. Uncertainty number one was whether Chrysler would survive. Uncertainty number two was which 750 dealerships were they going to terminate as part of the bankruptcy reorganization plan? If Chrysler was an ongoing concern and decided to terminate dealerships, it would be subject to the franchise laws of each state and responsible for everything related to closure like buying back cars, parts and providing adequate funds to close. But dealers terminated through bankruptcy court have no rights."

Holding the dealership together during those trying times took everything that Albee had. "John really bore the brunt of it." Georgia said. "At work, he maintained a positive attitude and kept the morale up as best he could. But when he came home at night, you could see the pain."

"We had already consolidated our operations," John added. "We were selling cars and servicing cars. From that perspective, we were still doing business. We were scared, but we weren't going to change. I had constant employee meetings. I told them, 'We're still here. We're going to fight like hell. Be confident. The people we have in this store today are the people we are going to grow with.'"

"If Chrysler had not survived, or if we lost our dealership through its bankruptcy proceedings, it would have put everything we had at risk," Georgia recalled. "In addition to the dealership, a lot of our personal funds would have been at risk because of the liquidation. It took its toll on me physically. I had to go in for tests. I thought I had an ulcer. Finally, I'm feeling better."

And what happened when they got the fateful news that their dealership would not be terminated?

"Probably just a giant sigh of relief," John said. "We were always confident. We had a great location, good numbers, but until the day we got that letter there was a painful level of uncertainty."

Right before they were taunted by all this business uncertainty, the Albees were almost sucked into the vortex of the mortgage crisis, a potential giant mistake that might have wreaked havoc on their lives with or without the Chrysler bankruptcy.

"We were looking to move into a new house," Georgia told me. "The boys had grown up and we had always wanted to be near the water. I was working with one of the top real estate agents in the area. She told me we qualified for a three-million-dollar mortgage. *A three-million-dollar mortgage?* If we had taken that, we certainly would be bankrupt today. We couldn't afford that mortgage then and John was making a lot more money than he is now. So we backpedaled. We dropped down to two million. We found a house that we liked in an upscale town right on the river, but the deal fell through. Thank God, the deal fell through. We would be choking today if we bought that house. Finally, we found a house on the other side of the river, in a town that wasn't as quite upscale for $750,000 less. We bought it and we're very happy with it."

Despite their good judgment, the Albees were not completely immune to the effects of the meltdown.

"We bought our current house with the idea that we would remodel parts of it," John explained. "We put a fair amount of money into it. As things began to get worse and worse, we kind of resented what we did. So we stopped and haven't done anything since."

"It's almost like our grandparents after they lived through the Great Depression," Georgia added. "We're shell-shocked. It's too soon. We're too nervous about spending thousands of more dollars. We don't want to be in a position where we're spending all our cash again. We never want to go through anything like that again."

It's early evening. A cool breeze wisps off the river behind the Albees' stately contemporary home. A few small sailboats drift by. Georgia and John are relaxing on their back deck, finally free of the anxieties of the auto business and the potential booby traps of the real estate market.

"We would have survived," John reflects. "It would have been ugly, but we would have survived."

So what do you think caused all your anxieties, how did the economy go so wrong?

"I think it's a combination of many factors," he answered. "The government certainly forced mortgages down people's throats. Consumers have accountability, investment bankers have accountability, mortgage companies have accountability. No one's completely innocent. Hell, when easy credit was available from the auto companies, we were lending it out like it was going out of style."

And the possibility of a recovery?

"I think it all depends upon how the consumer looks at it long term," John said. "There's always going to be booms and busts. We will crawl out of this. The stimulus package might spark a surge with maybe a little bit of a hangover afterward. I do think that over time, people will forget and start spending money again. It's human nature. Right now, though, people are not being frivolous with their money. They're managing it much more wisely."

How about retirement? I asked.

"We don't really have a specific retirement plan," Georgia answered. "John loves his business. He loves going to work. I don't see us saying, 'Okay, let's sell the stores and move to Florida.'"

"Our kids are in the business," John added. "So maybe they'll take over when I want to wind down a bit. I know at age 55 I should be thinking about slowing down but instead I'm thinking about the next growth opportunity. We're in good shape now. We have some cash, our stocks are starting to come back and July was the best month we've had at the dealerships in years. We're optimistic about the future. I'm talking to a lawyer next week to put together a plan to better protect our assets. We never ever want to put them at risk again."

So after a roller-coaster ride fueled by Jeep, which propelled their early success with the Grand Cherokee and threatened everything they had with bankruptcy, the Albees can finally sit back and relax.

Or not?

Their first grandchild is due in the Fall—*talk about a roller-coaster ride!*

* * *

Chapter 10

If You Can't Take the Heat,
Step Into the Kitchen

A n interesting blend of public and private sector backgrounds, ex-
police officer Dan Besso has carved out a nice living for himself with
his home security business and other activities. He is living testament to
the power of the pension—a power most Baby Boomers don't possess—and
he's also living testament to the plight of a small businessperson during an
economic meltdown.

* * *

"Reflecting upon everything that's taken place in the economy and
all, I'm glad I took the path I did," Dan Besso told me as he steps
out of his Chevy Suburban onto the driveway of his Rhode Island
home. "Today, I'm a retired police officer with a pension that increases
3% a year, I have health-care benefits for life, I run my own security
alarm business and I consult for a large insurance company. When I
graduated high school I either wanted to go into law enforcement or
become a chef," he chuckled, "I have to say what I have now is a lot
better than standing in a hot kitchen all day."

Ironically, Dan Besso, 54, could pass for either a police officer or a chef. Compact, stout, and sporting a crew cut, he has a soda machine solidity to him. If he stopped your car on a highway, you wouldn't want to mess with him. He passes the "Yes, Officer. Whatever you say, Officer" respect sniff test from the instant you set eyes on him. Yet he has a warm friendly face with round red cheeks and a glint in his eye that you can easily imagine under a white stovepipe hat as he orchestrates a large kitchen, checking on an array of sauces, entrees, appetizers, soups and soufflés.

He's one of those rare individuals who chose to step out of the kitchen and into the heat.

Besso's career path began in his teen years when he belonged to an Explorer post attached to the local police force. During the summer, he interned with the force, earning $75 a week. At age 18, he applied to become an officer. He was deterred, however, because a family member was a high-ranking local police official; at the time, Rhode Island municipalities were clamping down as a result of rampant charges of nepotism. Instead, Besso attended a small New England college where he majored in law enforcement.

"Growing up in the 1960s and 1970s was unique," he recalled. "I was a jock. At 17, I had to register for the draft. I didn't necessarily agree with the war protests. But at the time, when you graduated high school, you either went to Vietnam or college. I went to college. Was I a draft dodger? I still can't answer that question."

After graduation from college, Besso went to work for a private security firm. Two years later, he was finally accepted into the force, six years after he originally applied. It was in 1981, though, when his career destiny took real shape.

"My next door neighbor had a small home alarm company. I was able to work mornings for him because I worked second shift with the force. I would wire houses with all sorts of security systems, from the simple for doors and windows to the more complex, with motion detectors, smoke detectors and all sorts of gadgets. It opened up my eyes. In 1986 I started my own company."

Meanwhile, at his full-time job with a local police force, Besso developed another expertise. "I became an expert on automobile accident reconstruction. There's a real art to it. Many times what caused the accident is not always what it appeared to be. You have to have knowledge of collision dynamics to determine what actually happened. Through this analysis and knowledge we learn how to prevent future accidents."

The 1980s were important formative years for the adult Dan Besso. He met his future wife, Donna, in 1980, they married in 1982 and had their first child, Alec, in 1989. Their daughter, Tammy, was born three years later in 1992.

"We're very blessed with our children," Besso told me with a puffed chest. "Our son's a talented artist and he's about to enter his senior year at one of the most prestigious art schools in the country. Our daughter, Tammy, is a tremendous athlete and just earned a lacrosse scholarship to a small New England college."

Figuring out how to finance college, though, particularly for his son, Alec, didn't come without its share of anxieties.

"I have to admit, I didn't plan ahead. I didn't put anything aside for it," he recalled. "Then during my first meeting with the financial advisor at Alec's school, I had to leave the room. The guy had no idea what he was talking about. I felt like if I didn't leave I'd end up throwing him out the window. He had no idea about middle-class working people in this country, no idea about how tough it is to make ends meet. And, here's what really steamed me—do you know that if accepted students who were awarded financial aid elect not to attend the school, they don't give that money out? They put it back in the pool for next year. Ridiculous."

But Besso was never the type to let bureaucracy get in the way, particularly when it comes to his family.

"Here's my son, a very talented artist. He gets into probably what's the most competitive art school in the country. What do I tell him? 'Alec, sorry but you can't go. Your dad can't afford it.' Of course not. So what do you do? You take out loans."

Besso developed a statewide reputation for his expertise in analyzing traffic accidents, all while he was building his security business. He was even able to set up a statewide training program throughout Rhode Island on accident reconstruction. "It wasn't easy," he recalled. "But I met with all the large insurance companies throughout the state and convinced them that better training would, over the long term, result in safer roads. We didn't have to raise a lot, only $12,000 or $13,000, but we did it."

During his career with the police force, Besso developed another expertise. He became a Rhode Island Police Academy instructor in emergency driving. "Actually, that's one of the reasons I was able to retire from the force three years ago. I got a job working for an insurance company in Massachusetts teaching policemen, firemen and emergency medical workers how to drive safely during emergencies. I'd go up there about two or three days a week. They even gave me a 401K."

Multi-tasking has been a way of life for Besso since way back. Between working his shifts on the police force and managing his business, he's been able to carve out a decent living for himself, Donna, Alec and Tammy. "The home security business is basically a word-of-mouth business, even today still. I have a listing in the phonebook, I have a website, but 99% of the new business I get is through referrals."

So what's the secret to success in this business?

"It's about personalities," he answered, "but more so it's about craftsmanship, the integrity of an individual in the business. If you build a reputation, people will have faith and confidence in your business. My father, God rest his soul, used to work for me. If he didn't do things the way I wanted them done, I'd say, 'Dad, it's a reflection on me. Do it again.'"

"I've been lucky with this business," he told us as he snaked a wire through the wall of a colonial home in eastern Connecticut. "We've been busy. There's not enough hours in the day actually. We've been working six or seven days a week. According to a professor at Brown, the home security business is recession-proof. During trying economic times, people get more security conscious. So far, so good, I guess."

Besso has an increasing pension, a business that *appears* to be recession-proof (notice the italics) and he's a part-time employee of a major insurance company. So you would think that the downturn isn't really affecting him. Or would you?

"I saw it way before it was popular, probably around Christmastime 2007. "It began to affect people, particularly trades people. I noticed a lot of layoffs when I visited Massachusetts."

Besso explained that although his business was relatively healthy, the economy did throw some bumps in the road. "You can't get a small-business loan. It doesn't matter what your credit rating is. I tried to transfer my account to a different bank. The old bank was holding a $35,000 note for me. The new bank wouldn't extend the credit. I couldn't switch. And talk about stimulus money. Who's getting the stimulus money? I'm certainly not. There's billions of dollars out there, and I'd like to know who's getting it. Listen, I have to cover payroll, workers' comp and general liability insurance. Right now, the people who used to pay me in 30 days are paying me in 60 or 90. I have to pay my suppliers or else they'll cut me off. I've always been conservative in managing my finances, never used credit cards except for convenience. But sometimes I'm forced to."

Besso made it clear that he's no fan of the credit card companies. "You know, they dangle all these offers in front of you to get you in, practically twist your arm to take a card, and once they get you, they treat you terribly. You're two or three days late on a payment, what do they do? They increase your rate, even if you have a good credit score. I have two credit cards, I rarely carry a balance, but then I got a notification the other day that they reduced my credit limit. *REDUCED MY CREDIT LIMIT, can you believe that?* I didn't even charge anything!"

Between the state of the economy and the lack of credit in the marketplace, Besso sensed a general atmosphere of paralysis. "The oldest vehicle in my fleet is a 2005. Usually I replace my vehicles every three or four years. Right now I'm not doing that. The prices are down, it's a buyer's market. It's also a buyer's market in real estate. But I'm afraid to make any commitments. With the way things are right now, unless you have a money tree in your backyard, I don't see anybody doing anything. Even the traffic on the roadways is lighter than usual."

Predictably, Besso is not hesitant to dish out blame for the current economic situation.

"All of this is a result of mismanagement by the government," Besso explained. "Look at the Bernie Madoff incident. How long ago did someone file a complaint, three years ago or so? They dropped the ball. How did 9/11 happen? How did they allow suspicious foreigners to take flight instructions in Florida? You know, I was driving through Holyoke, Massachusetts, and what I saw was disgusting. Row houses, boarded up, prostitutes in the street. I thought I was in Russia or someplace. I said, 'Oh my God, do the senators and congressmen know what's happening here?' It's pretty sad. The town is crying poverty because they don't have funds for municipal services. I think both sides—the unions and the government—should make concessions so that people can keep their jobs and the city can provide needed services."

That said, Besso is willing to give the Obama Administration a chance. "So far, all he's done is hand out money, so the jury's still out. I thought the guy before him, Bush, was a real ass. He was already wealthy, his family would never be affected by a recession. Some people even say this whole mess started with the Clintons, that they forced Fannie Mae and Freddie Mac to make loans to people who weren't creditworthy. The Democrats gave everything away and what did the Republicans do? Absorb. Absorb. Absorb. Let's reduce the rate. Let's do this."

And how about the government bailouts?

"I'm not sure," he answered. "I definitely don't think we should bail out the auto industry. You know, I heard they were paying laid-off auto workers $90 an hour to stay home [referring to a jobs bank program that was begun by the domestic auto industry in the mid-1980s to encourage automation and innovation]. To stay home! No wonder why they went under. No one's paying me $90 an hour to stay home. I was a union guy myself, but this is out of control. You hear about things like that and it sort of burns you up. You know, they're bailing out the big guys because they're so-called 'too big to fail', but what about guys like me? I have a few state facilities as security customers. I've chased them for three years to pay back monitoring fees. But God forbid you don't pay them their taxes on time. They stick you with penalties. And, of course, they're exempt from penalties when they pay late."

Besso also points a finger at the downturn's common culprit: greed.

"I think it's a tragedy some of these bonuses you hear about. Not only on Wall Street, but right here in our own backyard. Do you know I read one of the health insurance companies in this state was handing out bonuses upwards of $100,000 to its key employees. That's criminal—the unemployment rate in this state is 13.5%. And then I read about this big pharmaceutical retailer dishing out $600,000 and $700,000 bonuses in an environment where people can't afford to buy anything in their stores. Why don't you lower the price on your prescriptions for goodness' sake instead of rewarding yourselves? I guess greed is ingrained in us all. We all want more but aren't willing to give anything up. But now it's different. It's not about fighting for your rights anymore, it's about fighting to survive."

Despite it all, life is fairly good for the Bessos. They live in a four-bedroom colonial split on a tranquil, wooded cul-de-sac in a beautiful suburban Rhode Island town on the western shore of the Narragansett Bay. Their acre-and-a-half property was tailor made for the summer with an in-ground pool and a deck that's perfect for weekend barbecues.

"Yeah, I like to flip a burger or two," he told me as he sipped a Sam Adams on his deck. "You know, it's not really Donna and I who this economy affects. We'll get by. It's the next generation. Alec graduates next year. What's he going to do? Where's he going to work? He loses his healthcare next year. How's he going to be able to afford it on his own? We need to get these healthcare costs under control. All these doctors are whining because their rates are getting cut. But I don't see anyone lowering our premiums. Where does all the money go?

"Knock on wood," he told me as he tapped his fist on the deck's railing. "We've been lucky. But, still, things can turn south at a moment's notice. Right now, my business does $100,000 a year in monitoring fees. What if people decide to stop monitoring? What if the bank calls in my note?"

Indeed, an air of uncertainty haunts us all, but we can learn several lessons from Besso's story. As a public servant, he worked hard for more than 20 years to serve the interests of the citizens of his community. At the end of his career, he was rewarded with a pension, perhaps modest, particularly at first, but one that would increase every year and was guaranteed for life. The pension gave him the freedom to retire in his early 50s and build his home security business. Today, as a small businessperson, he is on the front lines of the economic maelstrom—no one's bailing him out, banks are tightening their reins, his customers are stretching their payments, yet he has on-going obligations to the government, his vendors, his employees and his family.

"It's tough for everyone," he lamented. "Right now we pay real estate taxes of $10,000 a year. Upkeep on the house isn't cheap. I pay workers' comp for my business, I'm carrying loans on five cars and we've taken about a $200,000 to $300,000 hit on our house. What's left? But I guess I shouldn't feel so bad, everything considered. You hear these stories about people who've gotten laid off and are arrested for stealing meat at the supermarket. They've got to feed their families, don't they?"

Unlike many, though, Besso has a definite plan for the future.

"With us, it's a 10-year plan. We owe $70,000 on our son's college education. By then it should be paid off. The cost of living increases of 3% a year on my pension will be significant by then. I'll be able to sell my security business, collect Social Security and, who knows, the 401K on my insurance company job may even be worth something."

So what do they plan to do once they get there?

"I'm not sure if we'll be able to afford to stay in our house," he answered as watched the late afternoon sun glisten off his swimming pool. "Without the kids here, we may not need it. But I'm sure Donna and I will find somewhere to go, something to do."

With any luck, he may even find some time to do a little cooking.

* * *

Chapter 11
No Script

M any Baby Boomers had their lives planned out for themselves at an early age. While some succeeded in achieving their goals, those who didn't sometimes had trouble coping with a life that didn't turn out as expected. Others let life events come to them with no preconceived notions, which begs a question for Boomers: Is life better lived in pursuit of a destination or as a journey in and of itself?

* * *

"Retirement plan?" Scott Divak answered a bit bewildered. "Right now I don't have a firm retirement plan, though I'm trying to make things happen in my life to get to that point. I just turned 48 and I'd have to say I'm pretty bullish on my prospects, but I can't say they're clearly defined. I just lost a ton on my 401K, but I still have my apartment on the Lower East Side. It's almost paid for and it's worth around $400,000. Buying that apartment was positively the best thing I've ever done. I've heard reverse mortgages are a real scam, so I'm not sure if that's a retirement option."

Divak, a New York City advertising copywriter, is an interesting fellow to say the least. Tall, lumbering and philosophical, he has a completely bald scalp and a round face that's friendly and inviting. Quiet and understated, he has a tremendous sense of humor evident from the dozens of comedic radio and TV commercials he's penned.

"I consider myself more of a doer than a planner. I didn't even really plan out my college education that well, it just sort of happened. You know, sometimes I stumble into things. Sometimes they work, sometimes not. But I'm always resourceful enough to find the next thing to do."

Working without a script comes naturally to Divak. Although he describes his college years at a New Jersey state university as "un-noteworthy," he did stumble onto something that had a major impact on his life. "There was this improv group on campus," Divak said with a smile, "and the director gave us a fundamental version of Spolin [named after Viola Spolin, a schoolteacher in the Chicago area during the Depression who developed an improvisational theory that laid the groundwork for *Second City* and *Saturday Night Live*]. That's where I learned these proven methods of how to improvise on themes. That really occupied most of the time during my college years. Other than that, I was a communications major. I took electives in theater and toward the end focused a little bit more on English and art, but the improv group had the biggest effect on me. It gave me the idea to go into a profession that relied on creativity."

Upon graduation, Divak thought that advertising might be the best creative profession for him to get into although, predictably, he had no concrete plan. "I had done this big paper on advertising and I thought that might be a good place to start. You know, most of the kids had everything planned out in advance. I didn't have a clear direction, so one day I went to the Career Center on campus. They told me about this opening in the advertising department at A&P. They needed someone to do mechanicals and production for their daily print ads.

So I took it. Eventually, someone there suggested I take courses in art direction at the School of Visual Arts. So I did and put a decent portfolio together."

Divak's portfolio, a collection of ads he developed as a student at the School of Visual Arts, eventually earned him a job at a small New Jersey agency. There, Divak wrote and produced a series of humorous radio commercials for a regional savings bank. "But the guy who ran the place was highly unethical," Divak lamented. "Soon the place went bust."

Resourceful to the core, Divak contacted the personnel director for the creative department at one of New York's largest advertising agencies located right in the heart of Madison Avenue. "After she saw my book, she set me up on an interview with one of the senior creative directors. It turns out that he had heard my spots for the bank on the radio and loved them. Talk about luck!"

Shortly thereafter, Divak started at the agency. "Working there was a big break for me. I was 29 and up until then I hadn't done anything noteworthy. But now here I was in the center of the advertising universe working on big brands with big budgets and getting exposed to all kinds of things that not many people get a chance to do. And I loved the culture and the creative atmosphere."

But it was more than just that. Working on Madison Avenue really opened up his eyes. Divak reminisced, "You know, you think about the Kennedy family. Thanks to their father, Joe, they had an expanded view of what was possible. I never had that. I could have gone to a much better college, but I never even thought about it, never thought it was possible. Working at a big agency on Madison Avenue expanded my thinking that maybe I can do something special someday."

Divak established a reputation within the agency as an excellent writer of humor and comedy and was quickly awarded several raises. But after a while, he became disillusioned with big agency politics. "It got to the point where I had an attitude regarding my bosses that if they couldn't sell my work, I'm not going to try hard any more. There were too many gang bangs [fiercely competitive pitches within agencies when multiple creative teams are put on the same project and battle it out]; the stuff getting on the air was not the best stuff I was seeing from our group. And it was so political—I mean one day this senior exec is king of the world and the next day he's canned. Did he turn stupid overnight? It struck me as odd that the business was so screwy."

Divak ultimately left Madison Avenue to pursue something else. "I had this idea for a magazine, actually it was more like a guide. I wanted to put all the schedules for all the free events in New York City in one guide. I'd also include all the bars with live music and no cover. No one has ever put everything like that in one easy reference guide. I called it *The Skinny*. I had this thought, maybe a naïve one, that if I put this together and raised its exposure, some shining knight would come into the picture and help me."

As a result of hard work and an even greater dose of inspiration, Divak put it together, a long skinny black book with a comprehensive set of listings in it. Unfortunately, unlike his first big agency experience, luck was not on his side this time. His shining knight never showed up. "It was the summer of 1995, which was just on the cusp of droves of people going to the Internet. I had held the torch on the project for a long time. I lost a ton of money. I was 40 grand in the hole. I had to totally retrench. I turned into one of those bounce-back kids I guess. I had to go back and live at home with my parents for almost five years to pay back my debt."

In many ways, publishing *The Skinny* was a demarcation point in Divak's life. "My life could be cut into two parts, before and after *The Skinny*," Divak said. "Entrepreneurs are doers versus planners. I was bitten by that and, as a result, I took it on the chin. I'm willing to try it again though. To quote Deepak Chopra, 'You have to be married to the intention, not the outcome.'"

The post-*Skinny* part of his life began soon after when a former boss of his at the big Madison Avenue agency gave him a call. His ex-boss was now the creative director at a medium-sized subsidiary of the larger agency. "He saved me," Divak recalled. "He gave me a chance." But, once again, Divak found himself subject to the politics of advertising. After two years, the agency lost its biggest account and was closed down.

"I was one of the lucky ones," Divak said, recalling those days of mass layoffs. "I was only out of work for 10 weeks. I got a job in the in-house ad staff at a Korean electronics manufacturer in New Jersey. I always joke about those days, calling the whole episode *Gilbert Goes to Korea*. Our department was on a short leash. I found the corporate culture stifling, like I was entering a cage each morning."

Divak chuckled as he remembered a key moment during his tenure there. "I looked out my window from work one day and stared at this strip mall across the street. It looked vaguely familiar to me. Finally, I figured it out. It was from the opening sequence of *The Sopranos*. The Ba-Da-Bing was just up the street. 'Oh my God,' I said to myself, 'I work in *Soprano*-land!' Mercifully, they fired me after a year and a quarter."

Then it was back to the big agency where he started, this time as a freelancer working on a product that most creative people would rather avoid—tobacco. "It was a good-paying gig. I did it for almost two years. I was just glad to be back in the city and working with people who I could socialize with."

After those two years, though, the inevitable happened: The agency lost the account. From there, he went around from agency to agency and headhunter to headhunter showing his book, trying to get any sort of job he could, either permanent or freelance.

"After a while, I got the feeling that maybe my book wasn't accurately reflecting my abilities," Divak said. "Maybe I was naive, but I figured that they must factor that in when they review your book, like assume that you're 10 percent better than you are. It's funny, even the worst agency in the world wants to see a great book. They act like they're out to hire a gourmet chef when all they want is someone to flip burgers."

At that point, Divak came to a realization.

"My book just wasn't doing it for me," he stated. "Conceptually, it was a snooze. I figured it was worthless going around showing a book that would turn my name into mud. If you show someone the same crappy book twice, not only do they think you're not talented, now you're a pain in the ass."

So he decided to take action: He reinvented himself.

"I had never worked with the heavy hitters in the business, never worked with any of the creative superstars. So I decided I would take courses with the best people I could and put together a whole new book. It was sort of a risk, because spec books are weird for established industry vets."

If nothing else, his new book gave Divak a healthy dose of confidence. "Quickly I began to get positive reactions. It didn't catapult me to where I wanted to be, but it allowed me to stay in the city and stay in advertising."

Divak landed at a small agency near Union Square working on cigarettes and then at a direct marketing shop writing direct mail for the Army's recruitment efforts. "I hated it there. It was like I couldn't do anything right. Fortunately, they cut me loose after 90 days." Then he landed a freelance gig at Court TV in its off-air creative department writing copy for press kits, print ads and publicity releases. "It was fun while it lasted. It was interesting to be out of the packaged goods world. Compared to a tube of toothpaste, writing ads for a show about a bank heist is high interest." Unfortunately, though, company policy did not allow the group to keep freelancers for more than a set amount of time. Although they offered him a full-time job, Divak wasn't happy with the money offer.

Now he works as the only in-house copywriter for a chain of health clubs throughout the northeast. "On a typical day, I can be writing anything from a 'Sauna Out of Order' sign to a radio spot to a bus shelter. It's not a bad job. I get out pretty much every day at five. I get a free membership. Now I know tons about exercise and fitness. I'm actually down to my normal weight."

The center of Divak's universe is his 900-square-foot one-bedroom apartment on the Lower East Side of Manhattan. "The building has an interesting history," he told me while stretched out on the couch in his comfortable-size living room. "In the 1950s, it was a working house for the garment industry. The city built it for workers in the garment center. If you left the industry, you had to sell back your apartment to the coop."

Divak is pretty settled in terms of his lifestyle these days. He takes a car to his office each morning. Although he's not crazy about his company's dress code, the work keeps him busy and his day goes by quickly. His preferred form of transportation around the city is his bicycle, he works out most days, enjoys the offbeat cultural stuff the city has to offer, goes on Match.com dates occasionally, has a penchant for oysters and loves watching *Hardball* on MSNBC, especially when they do a piece on Sarah Palin ("the train wreck you just love to watch," he quipped.)

So how has the downturn affected your life?

"Not that much, really," he answered. "By last September and October, I was already full time at my current job. It was pretty much status quo for us. My company only had to close two gyms. My boss got the axe, but that actually helped me. They gave me his office."

How about your life savings, your 401K?

"All of a sudden it got cut in half. It went from $120,000 to $60,000 pretty damn quickly. That wasn't too good," he commented in this understated way of his. "You know, I really think the whole thing is rigged. Just like in *The Sopranos*, someone's pulling the strings. Problem is, most of us aren't high enough up the ladder to do the pulling."

Divak explained that aside from his 401K, he has few liquid assets. "Ordinarily I like to keep a year's worth of emergency funds in CDs—what do they pay right now, about 0.9%?—but I've been laid off so much I've had to draw on those funds. I think it would be wise to get some money back in the bank, though."

Do you think at your current salary and at the rate you're saving that you ever will be able to retire?

"My salary reached its high point in 2001. It was over $100,000. Each time I changed jobs, I took about a 20% hit. Today, I make $65,000. It will probably take a long time for my 401K to come back. At least I have my apartment. And in terms of inheritance, my grandfather owns a 12- unit rental property in New Jersey. I'm kind of hoping that will go to me."

What about the Obama Administration and the recovery program?

"Thank God that it's him and not the others. Truthfully, I was terrified that Palin was so close to the White House. I just thought the Republicans were far too powerful, did far too much war mongering. I remember studying Eisenhower's speech about the military industrial complex. He warned that it was a powerful self-perpetuating force, that when you have so many military resources, the likely solution to every problem will be the military, not diplomacy.

"Personally, I think it's encouraging that a black American is president, someone who is articulate, smart, not connected to the oil companies, willing to battle with the large insurance companies and very astute politically. He's such a different kind of American. I wish him much success. I find it exciting at a basic level to have such drastic change."

How about the government bailouts?

"I think 'too big to fail' is bullshit. Anti-trust is anti-trust. Those financial instruments that those guys on Wall Street created were bad news. It's like in the movie *Wall Street* when Martin Sheen warned his son about the perils of 'making money off money' instead of making money off of building something."

Scott Divak is certainly the type of person that psychotherapist Michael J. Formica referred to in Chapter 1 as "…more resilient, and willing to set aside their ego to cut corners and make things work." For Divak, his very lack of a plan is a plan in and of itself. He's learned to skip from job to job without affecting his spirit or self-worth. Where some see roadblocks, he sees opportunity. He can take being fired or laid off in context and with a healthy dose of humor. Unfazed, he accepts the inevitable for what it is and moves on with his life. He understands how to play the survival game on one of the most competitive battlefields in the world.

In an ironic sort of way, he's the master of his own destiny.

And if things don't always work out the way he'd like?

Simple. He'll improvise.

* * *

PART III

Lifeboats and Riptides

Chapter 12

(Actually, Chapters 11, 7 & 13)

We've examined the plight of today's Boomer from eight different perspectives. Indeed, the economic meltdown has had an impact of some degree on each one of them—even if just serving as an illustration of their resiliency and ability to cope. In these last three chapters, I'll try to look at some of the root causes of our plight and suggest some solutions, although some don't come without a fair degree of compromise, readjustment and risk.

Let's start with what remedies our legal system has to offer. Let's create a "composite" Boomer—stressed and strained to the max—to see what his options might be.

So here is our 55-year-old Boomer. He's been gainfully employed in middle management at a large corporation for the last 20 years, he's provided a comfortable life for his family, he owns a nice home with over $100,000 in equity, his daughter is a sophomore in college, he has $35,000 in his bank account set aside for her education (he and his wife have agreed to pay $25,000 of her $50,000 annual tuition and expenses), his 401K is approaching $400,000 and he and his wife hope to retire, or at least slow down and do something different, when their daughter graduates.

Then *WHAM, BAM!* The meltdown of 2008/2009 wreaks havoc on his life.

Suddenly his 401K is worth $200,000, his home is under water and, to rub salt in the wound, he gets laid off from his job—*rewarded* for his many years of dutiful service with only a modest severance package covering about six months of his salary and healthcare.

What does he do?

At first, he proceeds normally, living off his severance funds for the next six months. He seeks employment but finds it almost a useless exercise given the economy and the younger, cheaper applicants out there competing for the same spots. He pays his daughter's $25,000 tuition payment out of the savings account as planned.

So far, so good.

But now it's six months later, his severance money is gone, there's no sight of a job on the horizon, he has to start paying COBRA and the bills just keep on coming and coming. With no income, he can't replenish his savings account, which now has only $10,000 in it and will be depleted in two months. He starts paying everything he can on credit cards, he gets new zero-interest-balance-transfer cards and juggles funds back and forth, staying one step ahead of the posse, so to speak. Soon, one of his credit card companies re-evaluates his account and lowers his credit limit to below the current balance, then charges him a steep penalty for a late payment. He decides to take $50,000 out of his 401K, which garners a 10% penalty which is now down to $145,000, to hold in the bank for expenses. He starts doing the math and discovers they'll never be able to retire on $145,000!

The harder he tries, the harder it is to keep up. Without even knowing it, he's run up almost $50,000 in credit card debt, he's tapped out on all his cards, he can't get a home-equity loan because he has no equity and there's no paycheck coming in.

Is it time for that dreaded "B" word to slip into the conversation? Dare he consider bankruptcy? Is he doomed with spending the rest of his natural life with a big scarlet "B" on his chest?

To help answer these questions, I turned to Connecticut-based bankruptcy attorney Ellery Plotkin. First, he told me that the "bankruptcy stigma" is largely a thing of the past. "Since the recession of the late 1980s and early 1990s, when many people connected with the banking and real estate industries declared bankruptcy, the stigma has dissipated," he said.

Predictably, Plotkin has seen a tremendous increase in the number of cases he handles as a result of the meltdown: "I'm probably handling about triple the number of cases right now versus my average over the last 10 years."

Don't Look Back

"Declaring bankruptcy gives you a clean slate, a fresh start," Plotkin told me. "It gets rid of that big elephant in the room—debt—that has been sucking up all your resources. You can put your financial problems behind you and move on as a productive member of society and become a wage earner again. It also disciplines you to downsize and live within your means."

Besides the obvious shedding of debt, there's also a softer side to the benefits of bankruptcy. "When funds get stretched and the breadwinner gets mired in debt, it can have a devastating effect on his or her household, sometimes the marriage and other family members, and his or her mental health. Being able to get a clean slate and a fresh start definitely has a societal benefit," he commented.

Plotkin told me that people he represents in personal bankruptcy proceedings run the gamut. "You see all types. Some of my clients are at the end of the pipeline or just have a lot of credit cards or may be of low or modest income yet purchased a home with 100% financing and a variable mortgage. They only looked at the payments they had to make in the short term. They either didn't fully understand the terms or were overly optimistic about the future. The middle-class client might be self-employed and with today's economy their business is suffering and they can't pay their mortgage. Higher-end clients have bigger houses, bigger mortgages and bigger cliffs to fall off."

But didn't the Bush Administration pass legislation that made it more difficult to declare bankruptcy?

"That legislation made it a little more difficult to file for bankruptcy," Plotkin responded. "It put people under a microscope. You have to prove your situation. Before that, it used to be easier to file. Now the theory is that the government wants everyone to verify what they say." Plotkin went on to advise everyone, from the currently well off to those near bankruptcy, not to throw important records away. "Save everything," he said, "pay stubs, bank statements, bills, everything. You never know when you might need help and good documentation is a definite plus in getting through the process."

Can filing for bankruptcy help an individual modify his mortgage payments?

"There's nothing in the bankruptcy law that allows people to rewrite their mortgages," he answered, "but there was some talk about it earlier from the Obama Administration. Bankruptcy laws, particularly Chapter 13, are to a certain extent structured to allow people to stay in their homes *if* they can afford their mortgages."

Big IF!

Three Chapters. Three Choices.

Bankruptcy proceedings come in three flavors—Chapter 13, Chapter 7 and Chapter 11. I asked Plotkin to explain some of the details of these different varieties of bankruptcy and what chapter might be right for whom:

"The general theory of Chapter 13 is to help out a family whose breadwinner might be out of work for six months or so and the bank has already begun foreclosure proceedings. Chapter 13 allows the family to stay in their house and maintain ownership as long the breadwinner proves he can afford the payments going forward. The court then forces the bank to take whatever arrearage the homeowner owes and stretch it out over five years. So, in effect, the homeowner now has two mortgage payments to make—his normal mortgage payment and the monthly contribution to the arrearage.

"By contrast, Chapter 7 is straight bankruptcy or the "liquidation chapter" where the individual is simply looking for a discharge of his or her debts. Sometimes the person may be current on his or her mortgage but up to their neck with credit cards and medical bills. As long as they have a sizable mortgage, they can discharge their debts by selling other assets without touching the house."

Time out! What do you mean as long as they have a sizable mortgage? Isn't that counter-intuitive? Wouldn't it be better to have a smaller mortgage?

"In Chapter 7, a trustee is appointed by the bankruptcy court. That person's job is to sell off the assets and allow an orderly discharge of his or her debts. There are certain categories of assets, such as clothing and furniture and funds in retirement plans, that are exempt under the law and so will not be sold. In most cases, a trustee will not sell encumbered real estate because, if the mortgage is large enough relative to the value of the house, he won't be able to pay off the creditors from the proceeds."

Plotkin cited the example of an individual with a $500,000 mortgage and a house worth $500,000. In this case, there would be no funds for creditors. Even if the individual had up to $150,000 equity in the house, in Connecticut there's a $75,000 homestead exemption,

Plotkin noted, to which both the individual and his/her spouse would be entitled (if they held the house jointly) after the mortgage was paid off. So, again, in a case such as this, there would be little reason for the trustee to dispose of the house.

Chapter 11 is a term most frequently associated with business bankruptcy. "That was primarily designed for businesses," Plotkin told me. "Chapter 13 has caps on it—$330,000 of unsecured debt and $1 million in secured debt, which covers the vast majority of people. However, in more affluent areas, like Fairfield County, Connecticut, we have to consider Chapter 11 reorganization in certain individual cases." Plotkin explained that Chapter 11 is a less desirable alternative because it's much more elaborate and costs more money. Most significantly, Chapter 13 is a bit more user-friendly. Plotkin told me, "In Chapter 11, the creditors have a voice, they get to vote on the plan. In Chapter 13, the court forces the plan on the creditors."

The Ten-Year Itch

Although there are some concrete benefits to declaring bankruptcy, there's obviously a downside. "Once you file for bankruptcy, it stays on your credit report for 10 years," Plotkin said, "and you can't use it again for eight years. So I always advise clients not to use it unless they really need it."

Ten years on your credit report? Wouldn't that make someone persona non grata to credit and mortgage companies for the next decade?

"In a normal economy—emphasis on normal—clients can typically obtain credit again before the 10-year period expires," Plotkin answered. "Usually, the inability to obtain credit dissipates as the years go by. Traditionally, once someone files, they won't be able to get credit again for a few years and, when they do, it would be at a higher rate. But I've had clients who were able to get mortgages within three to five years after filing. The big caveat right now is the shaky economy. Right now I wouldn't be too optimistic about being able to obtain credit right away."

The Simple Life

But what does bankruptcy look like from the other side? After all, attorneys are attorneys, they see these things every day. They must be virtually immune to the emotional impact of bankruptcy or at least have developed a thick enough skin to minimize its effect. But what's it like from the perspective of the person who files?

Michael Benjamin (name changed) is a 56-year-old who recently declared Chapter 7 bankruptcy. A client of Plotkin's, Benjamin has been married and divorced twice, has three kids—two grown boys by his first wife and a young daughter by his second—and is a partner in a small service-oriented business.

"Before I filed for bankruptcy, my first wife told me, 'Of course, you're poor. You've been divorced twice so you already have a quarter of the assets you used to have. They've been cut in half twice,'" Benjamin quipped. "Then I had the double whammy of a lousy stock market and a housing bust. With my level of debt, there was just no way to keep pace."

I asked Benjamin if he was scared of the stigma of bankruptcy when he first contemplated it. "Scared?" he answered, "I still am. In the society we've built, an accepted notion of self-worth is based upon your wealth and your number of toys. So bankruptcy becomes not just daunting but also demeaning. It's like you've lost at the game of life."

Demeaning?

"The bankruptcy was demeaning because it left me reevaluating who I am and how I value myself," Benjamin answered. "It's an extremely scary place to be. You've lost a sense of security and you're left with few alternatives."

So how did you cope? Did you go to therapy?

"No, I didn't have to go to therapy, though I'm sure many people do," he said. Benjamin told me that he was able to cope by reexamining how he valued himself and what his sense of self-worth really means. "There are plenty of assholes out there with lots of money," he said. "I don't think that makes any of them a better person. On the other hand, wealth gives you a certain freedom that I no longer have, but it doesn't give more happiness."

Benjamin did not hesitate in reciting his litany of lost freedoms. "I've lost the freedom to live where I choose, my freedom to socialize as I wish, my freedom to travel as I wish."

Yet what Benjamin has learned through this process may, in fact, be much more valuable than what he lost. "I've learned how many things there really are to enjoy without spending a lot of money," he told me. "For instance, my daughter and I have rediscovered the library as a wonderful place to go. When I had money, I'd just buy her books or download them. Going to a library or a local museum gives us a new type of quality time together that we never had in the past."

Benjamin told me of one other big lesson-learned. "Going through all this helps you discover where your true support is and who your support is. It's funny how many people disappear once they find out you have no money left."

When I asked psychotherapist Michael J. Formica about this phenomenon, he concurred. "You don't really see a lot of 'misery loves company' out there," Formica said. "In some ways it's quite the opposite. It's a sort of social leprosy – if someone sees a person who is being drastically affected by the economic downturn, they tend to distance themselves. People are somewhat less inclined to help others out just now because they fear – quite irrationally -- getting dragged down themselves."

According to Benjamin, though, there is an upside to this whole dynamic. "Yeah, some of your friends get out of the picture. But then you find the ones who will walk with you and give you support and that sense of connection you need to make it down the road. Having no money can leave you in a black pit, a scary place to be. It's hard to go through that darkness without a flashlight. Your friends are your flashlights."

How about the actual bankruptcy process itself? How daunting was that?

Benjamin smiled. "The process was not that difficult because I had already crossed the hurdle. The biggest fear was in making the decision. I came to the conclusion that I had no other alternative. But once it came to the actual process, I was fortunate to have a good lawyer who took good care of me and held my hand throughout the entire process."

Hindsight being 20/20, would you do anything differently?

"Of course," he answered, "I would have been less giving during the divorce process, I would have reined in my spending that grew out of an economy that was ever-expanding and I would have chosen a job with a more predictable income."

But hindsight is, indeed, 20/20.

Back to Our Boomer

We've examined bankruptcy from an attorney's perspective and a client's perspective. So with what we now know, let's go back to our example of the 55-year-old Boomer at the beginning of the chapter. He has no equity in his house, almost $50,000 in credit card debt, $145,000 in his 401K, maybe about $35,000 still in his savings account left of the $50,000 he transferred in from his 401K and a $25,000 payment to make toward his daughter's college education.

Is bankruptcy a workable alternative?

First of all, if our Boomer was to declare bankruptcy, he probably made a big mistake by digging into his 401K, which would be exempt under most bankruptcy laws. But once an individual takes money out of a retirement account and deposits it in a conventional bank account, the funds are fair game. So whatever is left of that $50,000 he transferred from his 401K would be available for the trustee to distribute to creditors. If he were to go Chapter 7, he most likely could keep his family in their house (if he could afford the mortgage going forward), because it's in a negative equity situation, and if the house was held jointly with his wife, he would have protection up to $150,000 above the mortgage balance because of the $75,000 homestead exemption to which they are each entitled in the state of Connecticut.

But he's 55. Will he ever be able to earn back the money he's lost? Is his age working against him?

"I never advise a person to file or not based on age," attorney Plotkin said. "I do it based upon their overall financial picture—what their assets are and what assets we might have to turn over to the bankruptcy trustee. I also try to find out what their expectations are. Sometimes they have a choice, sometimes they don't."

Plotkin also commented that one of the key considerations is the person's employment outlook. "If a person has been out of work for six months and the expectations aren't that rosy, he might want to think twice about filing. Remember, he won't be able to file again for eight years. It's a difficult situation for someone at that age, particularly if they're competing in the job market with younger, cheaper candidates. They've become used to a standard of living that they're just not going to have in the future. It's a difficult situation."

How about his daughter in college? Would the $25 thousand per year that he pledged to pay toward her education expenses be exempt from the trustee?

"Unfortunately, bankruptcy law doesn't give any special priorities to people with children in school," Plotkin answered. "When you submit a budget under Chapter 13, the court doesn't allow you to deduct expenses for college tuition. It wants you to pay as much as you can to your unsecured credit cards. The general philosophy is to let the young person (student) get a loan or a job and pay for themselves. I've even seen instances where kids had to leave school."

So?

The good? Through bankruptcy, our Boomer can discharge most of his debts and most likely keep his house.

The bad? He will be left with few liquid assets other than his retirement savings. Without prospects for a job in sight, bankruptcy may be of little help long term, and he'll have to wait eight years to file again.

The ugly? Having to tell his daughter that she'll either have to leave school or pay for it herself.

Although one might have to journey through an emotional storm of despair, shame, fear, loneliness, frugality and readjustment, ultimately bankruptcy is there to help, to give someone a fresh start.

According to Michael Benjamin, there is, indeed, a silver lining to the black cloud of declaring bankruptcy. "A lot of good has come from it. I've found that I have some good friends. I have a new appreciation of spending time with people rather than spending money. And I've learned I can enjoy life without a lot of toys."

* * *

Chapter 13

Death Is Not an Option

In the advertising business, during downtime at TV shoots, we used to play a game called *Death Is Not an Option*. You would be given the names of two people (either gender, but generally physically undesirable) and were then asked the question, "Which of the two would you be willing to sleep with if death was not an option?" Needless to say, it caused many embarrassing moments.

Now we may all be playing *Death Is Not an Option*, but this time for real. With most Baby Boomers having little or no pensions, Social Security being inadequate to maintain their current lifestyles, the equity in their homes shriveling and their savings depleted, how can our generation ever hope to retire? Will we outlive our money? Will we be forced to work until 80, if we remain healthy enough? What would that mean for younger generations? Will our grandchildren be crowded out of the job market, creating all sorts of economic ripple effects? Will the only way out of the workforce be by becoming sick enough and poor enough to qualify for a nursing home via Medicaid?

To quote a well-to-do investment advisor when posed with the issue of possibly having to use a Medicaid-funded nursing home as a vehicle for her retirement: *At that point I'll go sit on the beach, do a shitload of peyote and just drift away into the sunset!*

For her, at least, death *is* an option—even if only in jest.

Many a Truth Is Said in Jest

But is it true? Is death an option for Baby Boomers who fear outliving their resources?

At the onset of the economic meltdown, there were, in fact, several high-profile suicides (German billionaire Adolf Merckle, real estate mogul Steven Good, Bernie Madoff scam victim Rene-Thierry Magon de la Villehuchet)[1]

But is this just an affliction of the high and mighty—those who defined themselves in terms of their monetary worth and couldn't cope with the shame inflicted by such a drastic fall from financial grace?

According to psychotherapist Michael J. Formica, the powerful and affluent may have more trouble dealing with the effects of a sudden economic loss. "We see a sense of helplessness and hopelessness more so with the wealthy [boomers] than with the more middle class [boomers]," said Formica. "These people have worked so hard for so many years, and now it's just gone, which leads to an intense emotional experience that is akin to grief. I've heard the word *decimated* used quite frequently. These individuals are very anxious and stressed, but often can't, don't or won't" – as in the case of the once-wealthy woman cited in Chapter 1 who is ostensibly ignoring the loss of her fortune – "see a way to rebuild their wealth and reclaim their social status. With middle and lower middle class [boomers], it's not so new. They're fearful, yes, but they've had the experience of intermittently living hand to mouth for years, and they're used to a little chaos now and again. This group has more of a capacity for thinking these things through and acting effectively in response."

Despite this resiliency of the middle class, I must admit I ran across a blog called *Greenspan's Body Count*, which keeps a record of all economic meltdown-related suicides and deaths. As of late summer 2009, the count stood at 106, a fair number of whom were middle-class Boomers faced with imminent foreclosure on their homes.

For Those of Us Who Enjoy Our Lives

But for the vast majority of Boomers, for whom death *is definitely not* an option, what, in fact, are our options?

"Outliving one's money is not a new worry, but it's exacerbated by having less money and net worth and by uncertainties concerning the cost of health insurance and care coverage," Dr.Ronald Manheimer, former executive director of the North Carolina Center for Creative Retirement told me.

Okay, but then how do we deal with these uncertainties? How do we cope?

According to Dr. Manheimer, "Coping strategies include serious efforts to establish and live within a realistic budget, simplifying one's life and shedding unnecessary luxuries, taking better care of oneself and avoiding unnecessary chronic illnesses…forming neighborhood or friend alliances for group purchasing of produce and other commodities, downsizing homes, reducing driving in favor of walking, biking and ride sharing, pursuing a deeper spiritual life that may offset disappointments over material loses, taking up yoga or tai chi or some other form of spiritual-physical discipline, and so on."

Part of the issue, of course, is the expectations set by the previous generation. All of us Boomers – at least those from the Northeast - have been preconditioned to expect a nice little ranch house in Florida with a lanai and carport and a lifestyle replete with bingo, shuffleboard games and blue-plate specials. Perhaps, though, when you take the long view, this vision of retirement is the exception rather than the rule.

"We've been living in an economic la-la land for the last 30 or 40 years," Jerry Shereshewsky, CEO of Grandparents.com, told me. "Ours is the first generation where grandparents actually lived *away* from the family. In the 1960s, 1970s and 1980s, the multigenerational household became deconstructed. Now it's going back to the future with more grandparents living under the same roof with their children and grandchildren."

Shereshewsky cited several factors that underlie this reconstruction of the multigenerational household. "Most people are going to have to learn to live and die in their own homes. The money just isn't there for what we would consider a 'traditional retirement' or even a nursing home for that matter. We also have seen a tremendous influx of non-Western European immigrants into the U.S. over the last several decades—Hispanics, Indians, Caribbeans and Koreans, among others. Culturally, they are used to a different household structure. They are used to a nuclear family encompassing three or four generations. The notion of their grandparents living somewhere else just doesn't fit within the cultural mores of these groups."

Despite the media blitzing us with news to the contrary, all is not doom and gloom for the Baby Boomer generation, according to Shereshewsky. He reminded me that, "55% of all grandparents who own their own homes carry no mortgage. So regardless of the value— up, down or sideways—they have a familiar roof over their heads and a relatively low cost of living."

Nonetheless, Shereshewsky sees a shift of "tectonic proportions" in the structure and lifestyle of the American family. People will work longer and work differently with a lot more part-time work. He also sees a re-prioritization of health and wellness thinking, with an emphasis on wellness, along with changes in the size and layouts of this multigenerational home.

As a leading-edge indicator of how living situations might change, he cited the example of an insurance salesman from Michigan nearing retirement age. "He bought a share in an 11,000-acre fishing and wildlife preserve in northern Michigan and decided to put up a few cabins and have the whole family live there."

Paul Arfin, executive director of Intergenerational Strategies of Hauppauge, New York, a not-for-profit organization dedicated to promoting intergenerational programs, issues and policies, adds another spin to the issue. "Because of prevailing economic conditions, there's more pressure on people in their 20s to continue to live at home. Many Boomers live in small houses or apartments. Then if Grandma and Grandpa have to move in as well, this further compromises the situation. On one hand, it's a positive. It keeps the generations together. Throughout history, generations have been dependent upon one another for basic life services, such as grandparents babysitting and nurturing the young children. Recently, we haven't seen too much of that happening. But as more generations live together in tighter quarters, it can also breed conflict." Arfin goes on to predict, "Just like anything, some of these households will have problems, and others will share in the rewards of this kind of intergenerational living."

Stay-at-Home Boomers

Given the current financial plight of Boomers, Arfin agrees that this generation will face serious challenges in being able to afford the lifestyle they've become accustomed to during their retirement years. "Government help is not on the way to address many of these issues. There are some programs supported by state aid here and there, but it's a patchwork quilt that most people don't know about. But Boomers are resilient and capable of solving many problems. More and more will be grouping together and creating self-financed type of projects."

Indeed, there will have to be new models of living if Baby Boomers ever hope to retire on their limited budgets. In a study conducted by Arfin's organization, several "alternative" retirement models were cited that allow retirees to stay in their homes and have access to the services they need on an otherwise limited budget:

- **Natural Occurring Retirement Communities (NORCs). As** the name suggests, these communities occur naturally as the given population within a community or neighborhood ages. A community is a NORC when 40% to 50% of the heads of households are 60+. The NORC essentially acts as a community association that provides services that the retirees may not be able to provide on their own for an annual membership fee.

- **Beacon Hill Village Model. P**erhaps the best existing example of a NORC is Beacon Hill Village in Boston. Here aging members of the community banded together to form a not-for-profit organization that hires a staff to coordinate services for the members. Services provided for an annual fee include such activities as grocery shopping, transportation to medical providers, geriatric care management and exercise classes. The organization uses its collective buying power to both vet and negotiate 10% to 50% discounts with local merchants. Additionally, the organization provides optional services to members, such as home delivered meals, handyman services and house checks for a discounted fee.

- **Community Without Walls. T**his Princeton-based community is a "looser" form of the Beacon Hill Village model. Fees are nominal and most of the services (assistance with shopping, chores and medical transportation) are provided by volunteers.

- **The Partners in Care Village Model.** This Pasadena-based village resembles a cooperative in many respects. Members of the village help to provide other residents with non-medical services (transportation, buying groceries, handyman work) and then earn credit hours that they can "bank" in return for future services or donate to another community member.

- **Home-Sharing Model.** This is essentially a screening process that allows retirees who live alone to find a house-sharing partner, usually younger, who helps financially through paying rent and also possibly by providing other needed services. Housemate Match in Atlanta, which provides extensive vetting services, has arranged for more than 400 matches with an average length of 2.5 years in its 20-plus years of existence.

- **The "Golden Girls" Model.** This self-explanatory model occurs when two or three retirees decide to live in the same home. Costs and chores are shared equally.[2]

"Part of the policy challenge we're facing," Arfin went on to tell me, "is we don't have enough assisted living facilities to meet the growing needs of people who aren't qualified for nursing home care, yet they still have care needs. Assisted living costs $3,000 to $5,000 per month and many people can't afford that. It comes back to finding more creative ways to stay at home while receiving the services you need as well as the increased care-giving capacity of people from 55 to 75 caring for people from 80 to 100."

Mutual Dependence. Mutual Respect.

Arfin cited another reason why it's important for retirees to stay in the community as long as possible. "Today intergenerational understanding is more important than ever," he said. "First of all, we're all competing for the same jobs. We see more and more middle-class older people stuffing shopping bags at Wal-Mart to earn an extra couple of hundred dollars a week. In Long Island we are finding it harder for younger people to afford to live here. This puts a greater burden on the older residents who stay. We need to make sure that there's affordable housing for younger people, because the whole community benefits from their purchasing power and their tax dollars, especially the retirees."

One of the most compelling reasons for encouraging multigenerational communities is the empathy it engenders. "Familiarity breeds understanding," Arfin said. "When people of different ages live together in a community, it reduces the likelihood of stereotypes and minimizes the possibilities of a backlash. It would be easy for retirees to say, 'Why should I pay real estate taxes if I don't have any children?' just as it would be easy for younger generations to say, 'Why should I pay Social Security to support the older generation?' They have to understand that the intergenerational groups are mutually dependent. We're all in this together. That's why we try to promote a healthy respect for all generational groups."

When the Moon Is in the Seventh House…

One alternative model that Arfin finds particularly intriguing, where retirees do not stay in the same homes, is Co-Housing. These developments are started by groups of like-minded people with common values, in many cases spiritual, but not always, who band together to build their own community of caring. Sprouting up throughout California, Colorado, the Pacific Northwest and Massachusetts, "they're not really communes, but something like it," said Arfin. "Together, the group finds property on which to build or rehab housing so they can live together. They develop their own system of governance, they have an active say in the site plan and the design of the houses. An important element is the Common House, where you typically have a large living room, dining room and meeting areas. This is important because the housing units are usually smaller so a lot of the community members' time is typically spent amongst themselves in the Common House. In some of these developments, the community breaks bread together every night, in others only several nights a week or not at all. The rules and lifestyle are completely up to the members."

Filling in the "Gap"

While some Co-Housing developments provide services for residents who become frail in their older years, Communities International.com is an organization more concerned about "the gap years"—those years between when Boomers stop their "formal" work lives up to the time they become frail.

Scott Adams, founder of Communities International.com explains, "These gap years used to be short. But now they stretch from roughly ages 65 to 85 or 90, almost a third of a person's life. That raises all sorts of issues; Boomers are asking themselves, 'What are we going to do? How are we going to be able to live? Where can we find something to keep us active, interested and involved?'"

Communities International.com provides a solution by building communities for people with like interests or pre-existing affinities. "The whole concept began in 2002 when one of my friends came down with Parkinson's. A number of mutual friends thought it would be great to form a community so we could take care of him and also take care of ourselves as we age. We looked for a piece of property in Sonoma County where we could develop our own community but ran into rural zoning obstacles that we couldn't overcome. Unfortunately, our friend has gotten a lot worse and is now in a nursing home. That could have been avoided or at least delayed had we formed our community."

According to Adams, human contact is very important during these gap years. "Loneliness is a big problem and once people get into what I call the 'aging institutions'—first retirement communities, then assisted living facilities, then nursing homes—it becomes worse. There are three things people need to remain healthy—exercise, nutrition and community. Being involved in something and feeling valued are important parts of a healthy life, particularly during these critical years."

Adams, an architect by trade, explained how community developments are formed: "Generally people who are friends decide that as they age they'd like to live closer together and look out for each other. Typically, it starts with around five or six people, then they begin looking for others based upon common values and economic considerations. Usually it takes about 20 to 30 households to form a community. Then they come to us. We help them find the land and design and build it, but all the decisions are made by the members. We have facilitators who help them bond and deal with some of the organizational and social issues."

Ultimately, though, it's not the location or the design of the homes or the landscaping that defines a community, according to Adams. "A community is defined by three important elements—connection, commitment and caring."

Community housing developments can span the economic spectrum. A more affluent group may desire to purchase land in Napa Valley and start a revenue-producing vineyard. Others might want to move to less expensive areas in the Midwest or Mountain states where they can own housing at $100 per square foot. But Community Housing is not about "retirement" in the conventional sense. Adams agrees with Shereshewsky of Grandparents.com that the 'move down to Florida and play golf and bingo' brand of retirement is mostly a thing of the past, perpetuated and perhaps contrived by insurance companies trying to sell financial instruments. "70% of men 65 to 69 and 55% over 70 are still working where I live in Marin County north of San Francisco," he told me, "not because they necessarily have to, but because they want to. You go from your work life to your life's work, doing the things that you always wanted to but could not."

In addition to the vineyard community, Adams cited examples such as organic farming, employment recruiting and a bevy of other service-related businesses where geographic location is not an obstacle given the power of technology and the internet. "Imagine a community of architects or graphic designers or headhunters," he said.

Habla Espanol?

An interesting and compelling spin on Community Housing is in establishing developments south of the border. "You can take your Social Security money and move to Mexico, Costa Rica or Ecuador and have a really nice life," Adams said. "I've spoken with many expats in Mexico and they enjoy the weather and easier life. The only negative is that sometimes they get lonely if they're by themselves. By forming a community, Boomers can benefit from the economics of living in some of these countries but also have a 'cultural cushion' so to speak."

Part of the Communities International.com business model is that each community is part of a network of communities with members being able to spend blocks of time at other communities—perhaps near family members—throughout the year. Instead of 'time-sharing,' members would be 'community sharing.'

And there's another big benefit of forming communities internationally. "Think about it," Adams said, "one of the beauties of the Baby Boomer generation is that we have a wealth of experience, talent and knowledge that the rest of the world would appreciate.

Maybe it's not appreciated here, but there's a good chance it would be appreciated there."

Back to School

One idea we discussed was perhaps buying and renovating a closed-down college campus, taking advantage of the institution's facilities—living areas, pools, tennis courts, dining halls, a gymnasium/workout facilities, the campus green—to build a community, perhaps where each of the members work in providing community services and maybe services to the external world, such as daycare, to help fund the community expenses. While Adams saw some merit in the idea, he thought that the typical college campus—even a small one—would probably be too large for a single community. But it could serve as a foundation for "pods" of many communities built on different interests and affinities.

Another idea offered by Adams concerned shopping malls. As some of the traditional department stores, the "anchor tenants" at the end of the mall, are forced to close because of the economy, there may be the opportunity to use the real estate to develop housing and an create a village where community members would then have all the resources of the shopping mall within walking distance.

Us vs. Them?

While the title of this chapter may have come across as a bit ominous, I find the content encouraging—and maybe even enlightening. Despite our relatively low 401Ks, our lack of defined benefit pensions, the declining value of our homes—despite all these miserable things—there are viable, creative and exciting alternatives for us during our gap years and beyond. Whether it be a multigenerational household, NORC, Community Without Walls, Co-Housing or Community Housing development or just mere frugality and more realistic budgeting, there are ways for Boomers to live dignified, affordable lives by banding together.

Another encouraging thought:

In an era where our institutions, particularly our financial institutions, have failed us miserably, causing the biggest financial meltdown since the Great Depression, isn't it refreshing to know that we don't need to rely on these institutions as much? By cooperating with one another—both across generations and within our own Baby Boomer generation—and by thinking creatively, we can solve many of the problems on our own.

* * *

Chapter 14

The End of the World as We Know It?

We've been through a lot, examining the economic downturn of 2008/2009 from many perspectives. We've looked at it from a broad perspective, then from the viewpoints of our five segments and then at a granular level, depicting its impact on eight different individual Baby Boomers from eight different backgrounds. The purpose of this book, obviously, was not only to discuss the overall impact of the meltdown on a macro level, but to examine its impact on individuals—our neighbors, our friends, our relatives, ourselves.

We've seen how Dick Shaughnessy was directly impacted by the economic forces that caused the downturn, costing him his job and most of his 401K. We've seen Donna Dellasandro, virtually penniless, struggling to survive in an ultra-affluent town where, ironically, some of the very people who caused her malaise reside. We've seen how Kurt Simpson's savings and life have been shattered to pieces, how Ian Stein's lifelong dream, one that he's earned the right to pursue—may have to be put on hold. We've noted how John Perrotti went from a trader making high six figures on Wall St. to tending bar at a neighborhood Connecticut bistro, how John and Georgia Albee, after a 30-plus-year crusade of building their business, almost lost it all because of the downturn's impact on the U.S. auto industry. Then we've seen Dan Besso and Scott Divak, both coping with whatever life throws before them—Besso supported by his successful small business and policeman's pension, and Divak with his innate ability to adapt.

On many different levels, the economic meltdown has disrupted us all—some dramatically, some tragically, some marginally—and that begs a question, a big question:

Is this torrential downturn casting cataclysmic shockwaves that will forever alter our way of life? Is it truly the end of the world as we know it?

Of course, we posed this question to our panel of Boomers and here's what they had to say:

- 10%—"We live in a 'boom and bust' economy. This is a bust, but there will be other booms in the future."
- 29%—"Eventually things will get back to normal."
- 21%—"I don't think things will ever be quite the same again"
- 37%—"I think this represents a fundamental readjustment of our economy and economic system."

The Enemies Within

To get an accurate gauge on what the future may hold, it's useful to examine the forces underlying the predicament of Baby Boomers today. Based upon my research for this book, I would posit there are four main factors behind the current plight of the Baby Boomer generation: a) the virtual evaporation of defined-benefit pension programs (based on studies I've seen only about 20% of the workforce is covered by such plans), b) the high divorce rate, which in many cases takes one economically viable household unit and creates two household units, at least one of which, if not both, is usually economically fragile (in most cases, the woman's), c) the extremely skewed inequality of income and wealth in the U.S.—the top few percentiles on the income/wealth scale suck up so many disproportionate dollars that they are leaving the rest of society with too few dollars to adequately cover life's necessities, and d) the boom and bust economy we live in—one need only have lived through the meltdown of 2008/2009 to understand the economic devastation rendered by this phenomena.

If you put aside the divorce issue (tomes, I'm sure, can be written on that subject), I believe the other three forces are inextricably linked by the underlying motivation of greed. The decline of defined-benefit pension programs is motivated by companies' attempts to improve their bottom lines so that those in the executive suite could earn their huge bonuses. The economic bubbles inflated by the boom-and-bust economy create an overcompensated elite class that is rewarded far beyond its contribution by an economic surge, which by definition, is part illusory, part fabricated and part real. This, then, further skews the inequality of income and wealth and fosters more greed throughout society and, as the bubble inevitably bursts, leaves millions of middle-class workers unemployed and millions of homes foreclosed in its wake.

In putting a final punctuation mark on this book and the plight of Baby Boomers everywhere, I thought I would examine some of these and a few related issues in more depth. Let's begin with the roller-coaster economy we've been riding on the last decade or so.

Boom and Bust: Creative Destruction

We've lived through the tech bubble. We've just survived or are barely surviving the housing bubble. Are we forever resigned to the roller-coaster vagaries of a boom-and-bust economy?

Joseph Schumpeter, a leading economist during the mid-20th century, developed the idea of Creative Destruction, sort of a capitalist version of natural selection. He described the inevitable booms and busts of economic cycles as an industrial mutation, "that incessantly revolutionizes the economic structure from within, incessantly destroying the old one, incessantly creating a new one. This process of Creative Destruction is the essential fact about capitalism. It is what capitalism consists in and what every capitalist concern has got to live in."[1]

Basically, Schumpeter saw the economy as an "out with the old, in with the new" type of process with changes in technology, transportation and competition, among other factors, wiping out the old economy and creating a new one.

The tech boom of the 1990s revolutionized the way we did business, stimulating an economy fueled by easy credit, venture capital and IPOs. Ultimately, the economy overheated and we crashed. Then just when we thought things were rolling along nicely again, guess what? We crash again. Only this time the boom preceding the bust wasn't created by real technological advances, it was at least partially created by the slicing and dicing of securitized mortgages, a more or less self-inflicted wound.

But How Far Should the Pendulum Swing?

I like to think of capitalism and the financial markets, for that matter, as a pendulum. Inexorably, a pendulum swings back and forth, most of the time keeping on an even keel. But every once in a while, the pendulum swings too far in one direction. For instance, too much wealth is created too quickly and the distribution of that wealth is way out of whack. Sooner or later the unsustainable bubble bursts and the pendulum swings too far in the other direction, putting people out of work, freezing up credit, pummeling asset and home valuations, and creating misery throughout the population.

Sounds familiar, huh?

Free-market capitalists think that it's okay for the pendulum to swing as far as it wants to in either direction. Bad businesses will fail.

Good businesses will prosper. The fit will survive. Out of misery will rise opportunity and the economy will reinvent itself.

In many respects, true, but at what price? Is it right to put good hardworking people on the street, drive families from their homes, deprive children of educational opportunities and limit families access to quality healthcare just because the rich got greedy?

We asked our Baby Boomers their opinions on what the role of government should be relative to business and the economy and received a broad range of responses:

- 46%—"I've seen the flaws of unregulated capitalism and I'm for more government intervention."
- 20%—"I am dedicated to the principles of capitalism now more than ever."
- 32%—"I think it's the government's role to make sure that all people have equal access to housing, healthcare, education and a dignified retirement."
- 9%—"People should fend for themselves. The smaller the government, the better."
- 45%—"I'm disgusted with government's role because it's rewarding failure and bailing out people who made mistakes."
- 6%—"I think Socialism is a good idea and it will help us solve some of today's problems."

Predictably, the extreme positions ("People should fend for themselves...." and "I think Socialism is a good idea....") received the least amount of support with the consensus being that the ultimate solution is some form of capitalism but with a certain degree of government regulation. Some of the things our panel of Boomers told me:

"I think government has a role in making sure people have access to housing, healthcare, education and retirement, but the solution is not to

tax the top 10% of the country's income earners. Before you know it, they will be moving to France like the English had to do [tax exiles]."

"I am also believing the government should step in from time to time to even the playing field and then get out again, except in healthcare—I do believe a socialized program is needed."

"I think the government should provide equal access to health care and education. Beyond that, let the market reward the hardworking and innovative when it comes to housing and retirement."

"While adopting a laissez-faire attitude would be disastrous, too much government control is dangerous. I am angry that the government is using my tax money to fund the foolish, greed-driven actions of others, especially without having established the guidelines to safeguard the monies being spent properly."

"We need to carefully balance appropriate regulation and disclosure with the benefits of having a capitalist society. 'Too big to fail' has to be addressed since capitalism doesn't work well when the normal pruning of bad businesses can't be done."

Too Big to Fail?

If allowing companies to become too big to fail is a big part of the problem, how did they get that way in the first place? Over the last several decades we have seen the consolidation of many companies in a vast spectrum of industries, from telecommunications and entertainment to energy and pharmaceuticals to retail and airlines, among many others. But what prompted this consolidation?

Surely, in some instances, there were operating synergies and competitive factors that prompted the marriage and created added value for the economy. But, in many cases, the deals were driven by our old arch nemesis—greed. If the early 2000s were the era of the hedge funds, the 1980s and 1990s were definitely the era of mergers and acquisitions.

Two companies, whether they were in similar or dissimilar industries didn't seem to matter, would be squashed together. The investment bankers and senior managements of the companies—those at the very top of the pyramid—would earn outrageous fees and payoffs as a result of the transaction.

Perhaps the most wicked consequence of mergers and acquisition is what it did to the human capital of the company. Of course, to make the numbers work and justify their outrageous fees, the investment bankers and strategists would argue that many employees in this newly merged company would become "redundant." As a result, many good people in middle management, people who had been the heart, soul and backbone of the company for years (as opposed to the investment bankers who were quickly in and out and the senior managements who are usually more transient), were put on the street.

The overall result? A larger company that was in many instances overburdened with debt, compromised in terms of its ability to properly finance its growth, bereft of a large portion of the good people who helped make it successful in the first place, people who truly understood the operations of the companies, and a few very rich investment bankers and senior managements.

Some of the biggest corporate mergers of our time have been absolute flops. Worldcom's growth—and ultimate decline—was fueled by a bevy of mergers and acquisitions throughout the 1990s. Time Warner was created by many mergers and acquisitions and has had its well-documented share of problems. Citigroup is the fabrication of, again, a bevy of mergers and acquisitions, some of which were enabled by the repeal of Glass-Steagall. The word *Enron*—the name of a company cobbled together through a fair degree of mergers and acquisitions—has become a synonym for corporate greed and mismanagement.

But it doesn't end there. The 1999 merger of Exxon and Mobil created an energy giant, a company with the largest market capitalization in the world; however, did it create too big of a giant? Could that possibly be a company a few years or a decade down the road that's too big to fail? Is the concentration of so much market power in one company in such a vital industry completely in the public good?

Leveraged Up and Shaken Down

Actually, though, the negative effects of these mergers were tame compared to the effects of the leveraged buyout—the financial tool du jour in the 1980s. In these cases, a corporate raider would target a conservatively financed, undervalued company, raise inordinate amounts of debt in the junk bond market, buy the company at a premium, then gut it and sell off its assets, use the company's cash flow to pay the debt rather than grow the company and pocket a nice return.

During this time, managements of companies that were conservatively financed with healthy balance sheets were so fearful they would become the target of a corporate raider, they would borrow in the capital markets to buy back their stock to make their companies less attractive prey. This action, while understandable, was anything but in the long-term interest of the company or the overall economy for that matter. The borrowing compromised the companies' ability to fund research and development and replace aging plant and equipment— real long term growth versus contrived short term financial growth.

Think about that: As a result of fear, companies were forced to foist short-term rewards on the financial sector (which already consumed a disproportionate share of income and wealth) at the expense of spending funds on technicians to conduct long-term research, and engineers and workers in the construction sector to rebuild their facilities. They swapped real gains for paper gains in a wicked reversal of fortune.

In a famous speech delivered in 1984, SEC Chairman John S. R. Shad, a longtime Wall Streeter himself, warned of the following:

"When a company has highly leveraged its capitalization, the consequences of even modest business problems, economic recessions or rising interest rates are greatly magnified. Shareholders, creditors and others have sustained billion-dollar losses as a consequence of the leveraging up of American enterprises. The more leveraged takeovers and buyouts today, the more bankruptcies tomorrow."[2]

History has a funny way of repeating itself, doesn't it?

The Inequality of Life

One of the underlying themes of this book is the raising of a key question: Why do we as a society allow an overcompensated elite class have so much control and wreak such havoc over the lives of the rest of us? To paraphrase Winston Churchill: Never in modern history has the greed of so few foisted so much pain and suffering on the lives of so many. But is this really true, is the distribution of income and wealth so dramatically skewed?

Economists use a tool called a Lorenz curve to illustrate inequalities of wealth and income. The diagram below represents a Lorenz curve for a theoretical society with perfectly equal distribution of income. Obviously, this situation is somewhat mythical—perhaps real only in the mind of Karl Marx—insofar that there would be absolutely no incentive to achieve above and beyond and thereby enjoy significant real economic growth for the entire population.

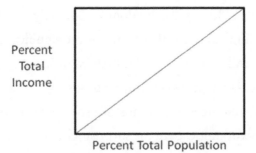

Percent Total Population

The Lorenz curve depicted below illustrates a more realistic income skew, the curved line indicating a skew toward the top percentiles. Economists use a statistic called the Gini coefficient to measure the degree of skew of income or wealth within a society. The Gini coefficient is simply the area between the diagonal and the curved line (the shaded area) as a percentage of the total area below the diagonal. A Gini coefficient of 0 would describe a society with a perfectly equal distribution of wealth, as pictured in the Lorenz curve above. A Gini coefficient of 1 would describe a society where one person has all the income (of course, this would be impossible to sustain, because the minute that person bought anything he or she would cause a redistribution of income, resulting in a lower Gini coefficient).

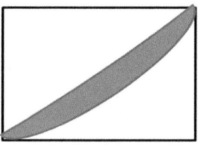

Percent Total Population

So how does the United States stack up on the Gini coefficient scale?

According to the The World Factbook by the CIA, the latest Gini coefficient for U.S. income distribution stands at .45, far in excess of any of the industrialized nations of Western Europe (Germany = .27, France = .33, United Kingdom = .34, Italy = .32). The Social Democratic countries of northern Europe are significantly below with Sweden at .23 and Denmark at .24. Underdeveloped countries usually have high Gini coefficients, indicative of a small, wealthy aristocracy controlling the resources and means of production accompanied by a vast exploited working class. Not surprisingly, the countries with the highest Gini coefficients according to the U.N. are Sierra Leone (.629), Botswana (.63), Lesotho (.632), South Africa (.65) and Namibia (.707). Contextually, the US at .45 is ranked between Cote d'Ivoire (.446) and Uruguay (.452) on the U.N. Gini coefficient scale.[3]

But that's just part of the story.

When you perform the same analysis on total *wealth*, the Gini coefficient for the U.S. is even more skewed, standing at .83 as compared to .71 for the U.K. and .68 for Germany.[4] According to some, this might be teetering at the maximum sustainable level of wealth inequality. But here's the scary part: Income comprises six categories—wages, rent, interest, dividends, capital gains and transfer payments. Most people at the lower end of the Lorenz curve derive income solely from wages and perhaps transfer payments (welfare). The people at the top of the Lorenz curve for income typically have incomes composed of all those components with the possible exception of transfer payments.

So what happens?

The wealth inequality serves as a turbocharger for income inequality, enhancing the wealthiest individuals' incomes with rents, dividends, interest and capital gains earned on their assets *over and above* their wages, creating a more disproportionate income skew as their wealth and assets are compounded year after year. The individuals at the lower end of the income scale have little wealth or assets and thus little supplemental impact on their wages and might even spend more than they earn, incurring debt and perhaps resulting in negative wealth or net worth. So because of this heavily skewed U.S. wealth inequality, we find that we are creating a steeper hill for the lower and middle classes to climb in order to keep up—in both income and wealth distribution. Heavily skewed wealth inequality drives heavily skewed income inequality, which then again drives heavily skewed wealth inequality and so on and so forth.

Economics Professor Edward Wolf of NYU drove this point home in a working paper for The Levy Economics Institute of Bard College in 2007. Wolf found that as of 2004, while mean U.S. Net Worth stood at $430,500, median net worth was only $77,900, obviously indicating that the mean was skewed dramatically by the heavy concentration of wealth at the upper percentiles. When you excluded a household's primary residence from the calculation, mean net worth fell to $319,400 and median net worth was a staggeringly low $17,000. Furthermore, the percentage of households with zero or negative non-home net worth grew from 25.7% in 1983 to 28.0% in 2004.[5]

The top 1% of households held 34% of U.S. wealth in 2004 and the average total net worth of these households grew from $8.32 million in 1983 to $14.79 million in 2004 (all totals expressed in 2004 dollars), representing a total increase of 78% and—more staggeringly—a 35.1% share of the total wealth increase for the entire population. The results for non-home net worth are even more drastic with the top 1%'s share increasing by 88% from 1983 to 2004, sucking up 41.5% of the total non-home wealth increase for the entire population.[6]

To put it in simple terms, it's not a level playing field.

And why is this important?

There are several persuasive arguments as to why such a skewed inequality of income and, more so wealth, is not beneficial to society overall. Professor Wolf cites two reasons why such skewed wealth inequality is not beneficial to society: 1) Many people believe it is simply morally wrong to allow such wide disparities in income and wealth, and 2) The divisiveness that results from such wide disparities can hinder overall economic growth. Furthermore, Wolf cites that access to quality education, and thereby opportunity, is more equally available in countries with less wealth inequality.[7]

In his provocative book *The Predator State,* economist James K. Galbraith equates economic power with political power and sees our boom-and-bust economy as creating a "particular kind of wealth, vastly greater than any other in our society," which leads him to pose the compelling question: "Are the people most favored by an inflating market also those best suited to govern the country and, by extension, the world?" He answers his own question by naming this new class of billionaires "oligarchs" and comments: "That word, which is not meant to flatter, reflects a general understanding that private persons with such wealth cannot be expected to serve any interest other than their own."[8]

An even more compelling reason for a more moderately skewed distribution of wealth is found in the book *What Is Social Democracy?* by Ingvar Carlsson and Anne-Marie Llindgren. To quote:

> *"Economic and social inequalities create bitterness, friction and confrontation; people who feel that they are badly treated by society have no reason to be loyal to a society that does not show them any respect.... It is hard to see that increased market thinking, and all that it has meant with changes in living conditions, has led to greater happiness and satisfaction; on the contrary, reports on worry, stress and psychological problems are increasing, not least among young people. Many of the problems facing the world today, in and between nations, are due to inequality and the tensions this breeds. Upholding the policy of equality and fairness is not just a question of ideology, it is about the necessity to create a more peaceful and stable world."[9]*

In the previous chapter, we discussed the challenge of spreading limited resources across the needs of many generations. One of the limiting factors, which indeed makes these resources truly limited, is the not merely dramatic but the *embarrassingly dramatic* skew of wealth to the richest Americans. Think about it, when 1% of the population controls 34% of the total societal wealth, that leaves only 66% for the needs of everyone else. If we sliced it in half and the top 1% only controlled a mere 17%, that would increase the total wealth available to cover the needs of the rest of society by 25%. That could fund a lot of medical insurance premiums, college tuitions and mortgage payments, don't you think?

A Striking Example

An illustration that best drives home the impact of the inequality of income and wealth in the United States is the example of Goldman Sachs. In July 2009, Goldman Sachs announced that it had booked $11.6 billion in compensation for its employees, averaging a mind-boggling $770,000 per employee, including administrative staff (you may remember some tabloid headlines that touted how Goldman CEO Lloyd Blankfein warned his employees not to flaunt their wealth).

Interestingly, the amount of direct TARP money that Goldman Sachs accepted was $10 billion dollars, almost equal to their total compensation pool (this doesn't include the indirect TARP funds they received through companies like AIG, which because of TARP, were able to repay Goldman 100 cents on the dollar on any obligations they had to them).

Although Goldman paid the $10 billion in direct TARP funds back, it begs a question *How would Goldman Sachs have been able to fund the deficit if it didn't receive TARP funds?* The answer is straightforward: They would have had to cut compensation and eliminate staff, just like hundreds of thousands of small businesses were forced to do because of lack of liquidity in the system.

I'm not arguing against the TARP funds. Based upon everything I've heard and read, we'd all be far worse off if we didn't provide the banking/investment community with a backstop at the time, but isn't it an egregious exploitation of the system to lavish such excessive bonuses on your elite group of employees when everyone else is suffering, particularly considering that some of Goldman's activities may have helped to cause the meltdown in the first place? What would have been the outcome if Goldman cut its compensation pool in half—now averaging only a paltry $385,000 per employee—and donated the other $5 billion to a fund to help small businesses weather the storm or to help the people who got foreclosed on?

Another interesting fact about Goldman Sachs is that apparently the firm owns a major stake in Burger King. I recently read an article that made an interesting point: If you took the total bonus pool of Goldman Sachs and extended it to all the Burger King employees, they each would have received an $18,000 bonus, which is in excess of the average Burger King salary of $14,000.[10]

So here's my point: Are we better off with the few making so much and the many struggling to survive. Yes, of course, there are different levels of talent and it takes a lot more education and smarts to put together an M&A deal than to flip burgers, but again I have to question the over-exaggerated skew toward the very wealthy.

The Goldman Sachs bonuses, I'm sure, bought a lot of expensive coops in Manhattan, McMansions in Fairfield County, summer homes in the Hamptons and on Nantucket, yachts, exotic luxury cars and many things I can't even imagine.

Wouldn't the money have been put to better use by bringing those Burger King employees up from poverty levels to income levels that begin to border on adequate, paying for decent housing, adequate healthcare and better education for their children?

Okay, that's way too much of an idealistic thought, but, nonetheless, the actions of Goldman Sachs during the meltdown (again, not to sound redundant, they were also one of the causes of it!)—their sense of "entitlement" to excessive bonuses even when they had to stand in the "bread line" and accept federal funds, then again compounded by their total obliviousness to the plights of others (again, this time, redundancy intended—plights that they helped cause by their actions in the derivatives markets!)—brings a new level of clarity to Galbraith's description of an "oligarch."

Transient CEOs and Today's Instant Gratification Marketplace.

In the olden days, CEOs were company men, lifers. They started at the bottom, got their hands dirty, learned the basics of the business—be it in coal mining, steel smelting, automobile manufacturing, retailing or whatever—gradually rose through the ranks and, by virtue of much hard work and a dash of good luck, one day ended up in the executive suite. By the time they made it to CEO, they knew their business inside out and were loyal to the best interests of the company, its employees, communities and shareholders.

Today's CEO in many cases, is loyal only to himself, his resume and the quarterly numbers, in that order.

In *The Predator State*, Galbraith tells us, "*with…the escalation in CEO pay, and the decision to link that pay to the stock market rather than to corporate cash flow, the top brass gained an entirely different class orientation. Instead of being company men, top executives became, first and foremost, members of a tiny circle of their own…corporate chiefs began to feel interchangeable; their credential was not as leaders of a particular enterprise but as a CEO per se; the credential for becoming one became, to an increasing degree, that of having been one somewhere else.*"[11]

In Chapter 2, I mentioned how the average CEO's salary had escalated from about 40 times an average factory worker's salary in the 1950s and 1960s to more than 400 times an average factory worker's salary today. Much of this relative salary inflation, as Galbraith mentions above, is due to the CEO's bonus being tied to the company's stock valuation.

Traditionally, Wall Street's role was to provide the financing so that entrepreneurs and innovators could build factories, railroads, fund the technology revolution, grow the Internet, discover new life-saving drugs and so on and so forth. Today, that's changed. At one time, business schools used to teach students how to run and manage companies. Today, it seems, they teach students how to run and manipulate the financial markets.

As a result, unfortunately, Wall Street has now become the lord and master to which all companies must pledge allegiance every single day or be smashed to bits. While I was an MBA student at Wharton, my professors drilled into us that the role of a corporation's management was to make critical decisions in favor of the *long-term* interest of the shareholders. Today, the majority of companies are managed to make their quarterly numbers, the results of which, of course, determine executive compensation. CEOs seem to spend more time meeting with Wall Street analysts than actually running their companies. In this immediate gratification, technology-driven marketplace, all the emphasis is on *now* as opposed to the future.

God forbid, some CEO might make a decision that would decrease short-term quarterly numbers to help ensure solid long-term growth. We see the same phenomenon in politics: Today, instead of politicians acting in our long-term interests, they respond with knee-jerks to the daily poll numbers. Imagine if daily polls existed when Abraham Lincoln had to decide upon the Emancipation Proclamation. Luckily, based upon everything we know from the history books, he would not have been swayed. (You might remember that famous, maybe mythical, quote after he had his cabinet vote on the historic proclamation— "Seven nays, one aye. The ayes have it.")

What our economy and world needs today is true leadership, not a class of professional transient CEOs who are loyal to no one except themselves, intent only upon making next quarter's numbers look good to inflate their extravagant bonuses. It seems so simple and straightforward, yet we still find ourselves living in an economy controlled more and more by the whims of Wall Street and a class of self-centered CEOs and our world run by a class of professional politicians way too willing to bend to the breezes of daily poll numbers.

Great Servant. Terrible Master.

Can we learn from our mistakes and create something new that insulates us from the booms and busts of Schumpeter's Creative Destruction, steers us away from corporate mismanagement and greed, sustains a more equal distribution of income and wealth both within the U.S. and worldwide and allows us to live decent lives, provide quality education for our children and achieve comfortable retirements?

Is government even capable of keeping the economic pendulum on an even keel?

Some point to Social Democracy—as practiced in some European nations, particularly in the Scandinavian countries—as a philosophy of government that allows for the productivity and wealth creation of the marketplace balanced with the needs of society as a whole.

In her paper *Understanding Social Democracy*, Prof Sheri Berman of Barnard College explains, "By the 1930s, Social Democrats recognized that markets and capitalism were not only here to stay, but were also an invaluable tool for producing growth and wealth. At the same time, they never wavered in their insistence that while markets made great servants, they also made terrible masters. Capitalism might be necessary to insure an ever-increasing economic pie, but it had to be carefully regulated by states so that its negative social and political consequences could be kept in check."[12]

Which begs the question, is a system developed more than a century ago still relevant for today's globalized high tech economies?

Berman answers in the affirmative. She sees a need for a system for "...the vast majority of people who recognize and want to share in capitalism's material benefits but who fear its social and political consequences. Since it was in response to precisely such concerns that social democracy first emerged a century ago, the best solutions to contemporary problems might very well be found in the movement's past."[13]

Are social democracies too far a step to the left?

There's a perception-reality issue going on here. While many reactionaries in the U.S. would declare Social Democracy pure socialism or even Marxism, that doesn't appear to be the case. Rather, the guiding principle seems to be a spirit of cooperation among key private and public entities as opposed to the more adversarial system we see in the U.S. In an interesting *New York Times Magazine* article on the Dutch system of Social Democracy, author Russell Shorto found that European-style, social welfare systems, "are not necessarily state-run or state-financed. Rather these societies have chosen to combine the various entities that play a role in social well-being—individuals, corporations, government, nongovernmental entities like unions and churches—in different ways, in an effort to balance individual freedom and overall social security."[14]

Yes, in a typical Social Democracy, taxes are high (52% in the Netherlands), but the government, sometimes in cooperation with other entities, provides considerable safety nets in the areas of health, unemployment and retirement. The Dutch have a quasi-privatized system of universal healthcare, so no one can be denied coverage or be charged more for age or health- related reasons, unemployment benefits are much higher than in the U.S., daycare is heavily subsidized and a lifetime pension covers about 80% of the population. In some ways, the tax rate of 52% is misleading; the top U.S. rate is currently 35%, Social Security and Medicare are additional, you typically have to fund your own healthcare without any of the safeguards noted above as well as your own pension plan (sometimes with company contributions).

The downside of these European Social Democratic systems?

When the economy is on an upswing, the heavy tax burden and some of the laws regarding employment (in some countries they say, "once you hire an employee, you own them for life") can cause a drag on growth. But maybe this drag is a good thing, maybe it can help prevent the economic bubble-bursts that reward so few and inflict pain on so many.

Perhaps the most poignant quote in Shorto's compelling article on the Dutch system is attributed to his Dutch teacher, Armelle Meijerink, regarding health care: "We look at the American system and all the uninsured, and we can't believe that a developed country chooses for that. I have a lot of American students and when we talk about this, they always say, Yes, but we pay less tax. That's the end of the discussion for them. I guess that's a pioneer's attitude."[15]

A New Normal.

So can there be a new normal? If so, what's the nature of it?

Needless to say, there are a slew of interesting alternatives out there. Close mindedness and lack of creative thought are the only obstacles impeding the pathway to a better future and a new normal.

We've looked at different types of living situations, from NORCs to Co-Housing to Home Sharing to multigenerational households and a bevy of others. We've seen how Social Democracies can combine a free marketplace while still providing a social safety net and basic services for the masses. We've seen how people working together can circumnavigate the stranglehold of failed institutions on their lives and solve basic social problems on their own.

Psychotherapist Michael J. Formica told me the story of an older middle-aged man whom had worked for years in sheet metal manufacturing. His knees were giving out and he realized he would no longer be able to perform competently at his job. Primed for an inevitable career change, he thought long and hard about what he liked to do. He had a passion for books, he concluded almost immediately. With much foresight, he looked for a career that he could work at well into his seventies where he could utilize this skill and passion. He went back to school and became a librarian.

As simple as that, he re-invented himself.

So there it is. Ultimately it's in our hands.

Just like Dorothy in *The Wizard of Oz,* perhaps we needed to endure a cataclysmic cyclone, a bumpy trip down the yellow brick road, with cohorts seeking brains, a heart and courage, to visit a wonderful wizard who asks us to battle wicked witches and flying monkeys to prove our worth, only to discover that the wizard wasn't a wizard after all. Instead, we discovered something infinitely better: Like our sheet-metal-worker-turned-librarian, we discovered we always had the capacity inherently, deep-rooted in our very humanity, to solve the problem on our own.

The solution is out there.

It's up to us to find it.

* * *

End Notes

Chapter 1

1. Steven Sass, Alicia H. Munnell and Andrew Eschtruth, *The Social Security Fix-It Book*, (Trustees of Boston College, Center for Retirement Research, 2007), 8.

2. Sass, Munnell and Eschtruth, *The Social Security Fix it Book*, 8.

Chapter 2

1. Thomas Phillippon and Ariell Reshef, *Wages and Human Capital in the US Financial Industry: 1909-2006*, (National Bureau of Economic Research Working Paper Number 14644, 2009) PP http://www.nber.org/papers/w14644 (accessed May 2009)

2. Michael Barone, "Wall Street Became Over-Dependent on Numbers, Lost Touch with Reality," *US News and World Report.com, Thomas Jefferson Street Blog*, 25 February, 2009, www.usnews.com (accessed May 2009)

3. "In Plato's Cave," *The Economist*, 22 Jan. 2009, http://economist.com (accessed May 2009)

4. House Committee on Oversight and Government Reform, *Testimony of Arnold Kling for a hearing December 9 of the House Committee on Oversight and Government Reform on the collapse of Fannie Mae and Freddie Mac*, Executive Summary, 2008 (http://oversight.house.gov/documents/20081209145737.pdf), (accessed May 2009)

5. William G. Domhoff, "Wealth, Income and Power," *Who Rules America?* Sept. 2005 Table 1 http://sociology.ucsc.edu/whorulesamerica/power/wealth.html (accessed May 2009)

6. Domhoff, Table 1

7. Stephen A. Holmes, "Fannie Mae Eases Credit to Aid Mortgage Lending", *The New York Times*, 30 September, 1999, par. 9, http://www.nytimes.com (accessed May 2009)

8. Eric Lipton and Stephen Labaton, "The Reckoning: Deregulator Looks Back, Unswayed," *The New York Times,* 16 November, 2008, para. 32, 36, http://www.nytimes.com (accessed May 2009)

9. Barbara McCuen, "Should the Government Use the Budget Surplus to Cut Taxes?," 2000 *Speakout.com* http://speakout.com/activism/issue_briefs/1328b-1.html (accessed May 2009)

10. Edmund L. Andrews, "Tax Cuts Offer Most for Very Rich, Study Says," *The New York Times*, 8 January, 2007, para. 10,11, www.nytimes.com (accessed May 2009)

11. Michael Wines, "China's Leader Says He Is 'Worried' Over U. S. Treasuries," *The New York Times,* 13 March, 2009, para. 2, www.newyorktimes.com (accessed May 2009)

Chapter 13

1. Linda Stern, "Killer Economy, The deepening recession may lead to growth in suicide rates," *Newsweek.com,* 14 Jan, 2009, para. 1, 2, http://www.newsweek.com/id/179422

2. Paul Arfin, "Baby Boom, Baby Bust: Is Suburbia Ready for the Aging Wave? Sustainable Community Development for Successful Aging," *Intergenerational Strategies,* 18 September, 2008, www.nyit.edu/academics/aging-arfin-sept08.ppt

Chapter 14

1. Joseph Schumpeter, *Capitalism, Socialism and Democracy* (New York: Harper, 1975) [orig. pub. 1942], pp. 82-85

2. Securities and Exchange Commission, *The Leveraging of America,* speech delivered by Commissioner John S. R. Shad to New York Financial Writers, 7 June, 1984, p.4 http://www.sec.gov/news/speech/1984/060784shad.pdf (accessed July 2009)

3. Central Intelligence Agency, The World Factbook, 2009 https://www.cia.gov/library/publications/the-world-factbook/rankorder/2172rank.html (accessed Oct. 2009)

4. World Institute for Development Economics Research, *Personal Assets from a Global Perspective,* Jim Davies, 2005 http://findarticles.com/p/articles/mi_6927/is_2/ai_n28319886/ (accessed July 2009)

5. Edward Wolf, "Recent Trends in Household Wealth in the United States: Rising Debt and the Middle Class Squeeze," *The Levy Economics Institute of Bard College,* Working Paper # 502, 2007 http://www.levy.org/pubs/wp_502.pdf (accessed July, 2009)

6. Wolf, pp. 8-15.

7. Wolf, pp. 8-15

8. James K. Galbraith, The Predator State, (New York: Free Press, 2008), 123

9. Ingvar Carlsson and Anne-Marie Lindgren, *What is Social Democracy?,* (Sweden: Arbetarrörelsens Tankesmedja/Idé och Tendens, 2007), 84. http://www.socialdemokraterna. se/upload/Internationellt/Other%20Languages/ WhatisSocialDemocracy.pdf (accessed Sept. 2009)

10. "King Size Combo: What Burger King and Goldman Sachs are Costing our Country," Service Employees International Union, 2009

11. Galbraith, p. 102

12. Sheri Berman, "Understanding Social Democracy," p. 22 (Barnard College, Columbia University), 22. http://www8.georgetown.edu/centers/cdacs/bermanpaper.pdf

13. Berman, p.23

14. Russell Shorto, "Going Dutch – How I Learned to Love the European Welfare State," The New York Times Magazine, 3 May, 2009, para 28, www.newyorktimes.com (accessed Oct. 2009)

15. Shorto, para 25

Index

BUY A SHARE OF THE FUTURE IN YOUR COMMUNITY

These certificates make great holiday, graduation and birthday gifts that can be personalized with the recipient's name. The cost of one S.H.A.R.E. or one square foot is $54.17. The personalized certificate is suitable for framing and will state the number of shares purchased and the amount of each share, as well as the recipient's name. The home that you participate in "building" will last for many years and will continue to grow in value.

Here is a sample SHARE certificate:

HABITAT FOR HUMANITY

THIS CERTIFIES THAT

YOUR NAME HERE

HAS INVESTED IN A HOME FOR A DESERVING FAMILY

1985-2005

TWENTY YEARS OF BUILDING FUTURES IN OUR COMMUNITY ONE HOME AT A TIME

1200 SQUARE FOOT HOUSE @ $65,000 = $54.17 PER SQUARE FOOT
This certificate represents a tax deductible donation. It has no cash value.

YES, I WOULD LIKE TO HELP!

I support the work that Habitat for Humanity does and I want to be part of the excitement! As a donor, I will receive periodic updates on your construction activities but, more importantly, I know my gift will help a family in our community realize the dream of homeownership. **I would like to SHARE in your efforts against substandard housing in my community!** *(Please print below)*

PLEASE SEND ME _____ SHARES at $54.17 EACH = $ $_____

In Honor Of: _____

Occasion: (Circle One)   HOLIDAY   BIRTHDAY   ANNIVERSARY

     OTHER: _____

Address of Recipient: _____

Gift From: _____   *Donor Address:* _____

Donor Email: _____

I AM ENCLOSING A CHECK FOR $ $_____ PAYABLE TO HABITAT FOR HUMANITY OR PLEASE CHARGE MY VISA OR MASTERCARD *(CIRCLE ONE)*

Card Number _____ Expiration Date: _____

Name as it appears on Credit Card _____ Charge Amount $ _____

Signature _____

Billing Address _____

Telephone # Day _____ Eve _____

PLEASE NOTE: Your contribution is tax-deductible to the fullest extent allowed by law.
Habitat for Humanity • P.O. Box 1443 • Newport News, VA 23601 • 757-596-5553
www.HelpHabitatforHumanity.org